REGISTER
OF
FREE NEGROES

AND ALSO OF

DOWER SLAVES, BRUNSWICK COUNTY, VIRGINIA,

1803–1850

Transcribed and Indexed
by
Frances Holloway Wynne

HERITAGE BOOKS
2026

HERITAGE BOOKS

AN IMPRINT OF HERITAGE BOOKS, INC.

Books, CDs, and more—Worldwide

For our listing of thousands of titles see our website
at
www.HeritageBooks.com

A Facsimile Reprint
Published 2026 by
HERITAGE BOOKS, INC.
Publishing Division
5810 Ruatan Street
Berwyn Heights, MD 20740

Fairfax, Virginia
1983

— Publisher's Notice —
In reprints such as this, it is often not possible to remove blemishes from the original. We feel the contents of this book warrant its reissue despite these blemishes and hope you will agree and read it with pleasure.

International Standard Book Number
Paperbound: 978-0-7884-2763-3

TABLE of CONTENTS

Dedication

This book would never have been completed without the untiring elp and devotion of my husband and my mother. To say only thank ou seems inadequate, no matter how sincerely I feel it, but I shall ay it hoping they know what I mean. This is for you. Thank you.

ACKNOWLEDGEMENTS

This project was started with high hopes for an early completion. As time passed, though, it became evident that ease of operation would not be a characteristic. Mr. and Mrs. James Dent Walker gave their time, equipment, and encouragement unstintingly along with morale boosting when problems looked unsurmountable.

Mr. M. Henry Turnbull, Clerk of the Court of Brunswick County, made the records available to me on a number of occasions, without hesitation. His staff was more than helpful. Mrs. Jean Clay, Mrs. Lillian Kidd, and Mr. Julian Scarborough kept what could have become a nightmare because of a series of unpredictable misadventures from becoming such.

To my friend and typist Mrs. Anita Whitley goes a special thank you because of the patience and forebearance she displayed. I appreciate her help more than I can ever repay.

Frances Holloway Wynne
9151 Hermosa Drive
Fairfax, Virginia
June 13, 1983

Introduction

The rationale behind the registration of free Negroes in Virginia had its origin in 1620 with the introduction of the first Negroes into the state by the masters of a Dutch ship (1). Both Shepherd and Hening give the background and feeling of the times as well as the laws. Inasmuch as the laws of the state from 1619 reflect the attitude of the legislators and society in general toward slaves as well as indentured servants, it is interesting to note how little importance was attached to them. Slaves had been determined to be property. Only with each new generation, were laws added or changed that affected the institution. By 1662 the state determined the status of a child by the condition of the mother; if the mother were free, the child was free; if the mother were a slave, the child was a slave. The status of the father did not enter into any of the determination. The April 1691 act for suppressing outlying slaves states strong laws against miscegenation (2):

> . . . And for prevention of that abominable mixture and spurious issue which hereafter may increase in this dominion as well by negroes, mulattos, and Indians intermarrying with the English, or other white women, as by their unlawfull accompanying with one another . . . that whatsoever English or other white man or woman being free shall intermarry with a negroe, mulatto, or Indian man or woman bond or free shall within three months after such marriage be banished and removed from his dominion forever,. . .

If the English woman had an illegitimate child by any Negro or mulatto, she would be fined fifteen pounds sterling, and the child bound out until age thirty. If she were a servant, she would be sold after her original time had expired for an additional period of five years. Any money from sale of mother or child was to be divided equally among the government, the parish and the informant who reported the case to the authorities.

In 1705 the law was changed to a prison term of six months and a fine of ten pounds current money for miscegenation. Even the minister who performed the ceremony was fined the staggering amount of ten thousand pounds of tobacco. The 1705 law was also interesting in that it was the first time any mention had been made of a registration of free servants. In order that no servant whose indenture had been satisfied could be accused of being a runaway, a certificate from the clerk of the court in the county where he or she had served was necessary so that the prospective employer would know he could hire without danger or violation of the law against hiring someone else's servants. The employer was to hold the certificate for the duration of the contract only (3).

It was not impossible for a slave to earn freedom. One such incident occurred in 1710 (4):

> WHEREAS a Negro Slave, named Will, belonging to Robert Ruffin,of the County of Surry, was signally serviceable in discovering a conspiracy of diverse negros in the said county, for levying war in the colony, for a reward of his fidelity and for encouragement of such services,
>
> Be it enacted, by the Lieutenant-Governor, Council and Burgesses, of this General Assembly, and it is hereby enacted, by the authority of the same,That the said Negro Will, is and shall be forever hereafter free from his slavery, and shall be esteemed, deemed and taken, and is hereby declared to be a free man, and shall enjoy and have all the liberties, privileges and immunitys of or to a free negro belonging, and shall inhabit, continue and be within this colony and dominion of Virginia, if he think fit to continue therein.
>
> And be it further enacted, by the authority aforesaid, that the sum of forty pounds sterling be paid and satifyed to the said Robert Ruffin for the price of the said negro Will, made free as above said, by Elizabeth Harrison, widow and administratrix of the goods and chattles, rights and credits, of Benjamin Harrison, the younger gentleman, decd. late treasurer of the public impositions of this colony, out of the public moneys in her hands.

In 1723 even though certain instances for freedom were a part of the general statutes, there were severe penalties for those who manumitted or emancipated for any other reason (5):

> And be it further enacted, by the authority aforesaid, That no negro, mulatto, or Indian slaves, shall be set free, upon any pretence whatsoever, except for some meritorious services, to be adjudged

> and allowed by the governor and council, for the time being, and a licence thereupon first had and abtained. -- And that, where any slave shall be set free by his master or owner, otherwise than is herein before directed, it shall and may be lawful for the church wardens of the parish, wherein much negro, mulatto, or indian, shall reside for the space of one month, next after his or her being set free, and they are hereby authorized and required, to take up, and sell the said negro, mulatto, or indian, as slaves, at the next court held for the said county, by public outcry; and that the monies arising by such sale, shall be applied to the use of the said parish, by the vestry thereof.

It was not until fifty-five years later on 5 October 1778 that an act was passed prohibiting slave trade in Virginia (6). Anyone importing slaves after that date was subject to a thousand pound fine for each slave imported; buyer or seller could be fined five hundred pounds each; and the imported slave could become free. Now that further importation was illegal, manumission came under scrutiny again (7). It was decided that after May 6, 1782, it would be lawful:

> . . . for any person, by his or her last will and testament, or by any other instrument in writing, under his or her hand and seal, attested and proved in the county court by two witnesses, or acknowledged by the party in the court of the county where he or she resides, to emancipate and set free, his or her slaves, or any of them, who shall thereupon be entirely and fully discharged from the performance on any contract entered into during servitude, and enjoy as full freedom as if they had been particularly named and freed by this act.

At the end of the War of the Revolution, emancipation for military service was added as a basis for freedom. The Act of 1778 was more bravado than anything else since there was no resolution of the conflict between Great Britain and America until 1783. The generation, having gambled so much on freedom from England and won, declared (after stopping the slave trade albeit seven years earlier than they actually had any legal right to do) that the only slaves in the commonwealth would be those who were slaves on 17 October 1785 and any increase of those that were female. All others brought in after that date would be freed after one year.

Registration came into being, after a fashion, fifteen years later in December of 1800 when the legislature directed the Commissioner of Revenue of each county to return a complete list of free Negroes or mulattos by name; sex; place of abode; trade, occupation, or calling; and to affix a copy to the court house door, with another placed for safekeeping in the office. Failure to do so would be a twenty dollar fine. If any Negro so registered should move to another county, the magistrate of the county was to examine the Negro to determine his status--free or slave. Anyone unemployed could be considered a vagrant. Nothing more was done until 1805 when it was decreed that any slave brought into the state would be free after one year. If any emancipated slave remained in the state without permission of the county or state for more than a year after emancipation, he would forfeit his right to freedom and could be apprehended and resold for the benefit of the poor (8).

It is at this time that the following registrations take up. The two volumes were found in the Court house in Brunswick County at Lawrenceville, Virginia, and transcrived verbatim, maintaining the original spelling, punctuation, and wording. The first volume of 101 registrations, starting in 1803, was misplaced for many years and found only lately in the back of another, different book. The second volume starts with the registration 102 and continues more or less consecutively through number 551. There are some vagaries of numbering that should be explained. Some of the certificates showing registration of different people are for some unknown reason numbered with the same number. In one place the numbering is in error by 100. Any number that is a duplicate is marked with an asterisk and so noted in the text in parentheses.

The certificates reflect the laws governing manumissions. Either the black was free by virtue of a deed, a court suit, or by birth to a free mother. In some instances it was not clear by the wording how freedom was attained. One might suspect that the majority or registrations would come from ex-slaves freed either by last will and testament or by deed. In the first book of registrations covering the first five months of 1820, such is the case. Of all the ex-slaves registered before June 1820 31% show freedom by last will and testament, 33% by deed of emancipation, and only 21% by free birth. Book 2, starting with the August court of 1820, shows quite a difference: 11% were free by will, 11% by deed, and 74% by free birth. Overall, 64% of the registrations for the County show freedom by birth. Appendix G shows a statistical breakdown of registrations by origin of freedom, numbers in each category, and percentages.

There are inconsistencies evident as one studies the registrations. Aside from the differences in wording, indicating a change in person writing, the lack of consistency would seem to indicate an apparent disregard for the law, letter or spirit. In some certificates, permission to remain in the state circumvents the intent to have freed slaves leave. If the purpose of the law was to keep free slaves from causing trouble among those not yet freed, it would seem that permission to stay had to be based on something greater than the possibility of insurrection. While some of the early certificates show occupations, most of the later ones do not. It would seem that people possessing skills vital to the community's economy were permitted to remain. No doubt trouble makers were encouraged to leave.

The people registered as shown in these two books should have appeared in the federal censuses and vice versa. Appendices A, B, C, and D show free black heads of households for the decennial years 1810 through 1840. All names listed in those censuses do not show up in the registrations, nor do all registrants appear on the census rolls. The latter instance can be accounted for in that many listed as free black were not heads of households but were shown living with white families, consequently they would not appear by their own names. An explanation for the former instance--free blacks with no registrations is open to conjecture--another instance of inconsistency or a lack of interest in upholding the letter of the law?

Appendix E gives a list of Clerks of the Court with years of their tenure and Justices of the peace by the years in which their names appear. Appendix F shows graphically in five year increments the number of registrations. The sudden increase between 1821 and 1825 is attributable to the emancipation by Edward Dromgoole of a large number of slaves. Equally dramatic is the rapid decrease shortly thereafter. A partial explanation is the concern felt immediately after the Nat Turner insurrection in 1831.

Appendix H shows the formation of the counties surrounding Brunswick and the dates of their formation and parent counties. In adjacent counties, additional information on freedmen missing in later Brunswick records could be found, just as ex-slaves freed in other counties appeared in Brunswick. Because there was so much interaction between counties, the adjacent and nearby North Carolina counties are shown as well.

It is unfortunate that the registrations were not recorded beyond 1850, or if they were, that they are not extant in the Court house. One can but wonder if the last eleven years of the practice of registrations would yield so many puzzling and interesting questions as the first years did. The reflections of a society's attitudes and the growth of its social conscience are clearly evident from the minutest description of every scar and mark on the one hand to a disregard of the law entirely on the other. The practice of registration in general ceased in 1861 with the advent of the War. Does the lack of registrations after 1850 signal the growing concern for more pressing problems? Were the certificates recorded in other books and subsequently lost as Book 1 had been for so many years? Perhaps in time answers will appear.

Using the Index

The names of registrants without surnames appears at the beginning of the general index. Some of these names appear in the censuses with surnames, but no attempt was made here to assign a surname if none appeared on the certificate. In some places it is evident that the registrants took the name of the emancipator. In event a registrant has the same name as an emancipator, every effort has been made to put the names of registrant ahead of the emancipator or witness. As asterisk after a name indicates an emancipator or witness. Any name appearing on a page numbered higher than 190 will appear in an appendix.

Counties other than Brunswick, as well as cities specifically named, and occupations have been indexed separately. Since all entries are spelled as they appear in the registrations, it will be necessary to check all possible spellings to be certain of reading all entries for a particular name.

NOTES

1. HENING, WILLIAM WALLER, *The Statutes at Large;, Being a Collection of All the Laws of Virginia, from the first Session of the Legislature in the Years 1619,* 1823, Vol. 1, p. 146 Note.

2. HENING, *op. cit.,* Vol. 3, p. 86

3. *Ibid.,* p. 453.

4. *Ibid.,* p. 537.

5. HENING, *op. cit.,* Vol. 4, p. 132.

6. HENING, *op. cit.,* Vol. 9, p. 471.

7. HENING, *op. cit.,* Vol. 11, p. 39.

8. SHEPHERD, SAMUEL, *The Statutes at Large of Virginia, from October Session 1792, to December Session 1806, Inclusive, in Three Volumes, (New Series,) Being a Contiunation of Hening;* 1835, Vol. 3, p. 252.

Brunswick County to wit I do hereby certify that TREAL a black man of a yellowish complection about 54 years of age about five feet 10 or 11 Inches high no scars percievable on his face hand or arms has a mole over the right eye brow who it appears from a certificate from the clerk of Southampton Court was emancipated by THOS PORTER of the said County 20 January. Given under my hand 29 Nov 1803.

Register No. 1 & cop'd H. Hill CLC

58 years of age Renewed 4th Octr. 1808

=====

Brunswick County to wit I do hereby certify that the bearer hereof JACOB a black man about thirty five years of age of a black complection about 5 feet 8 or 9 inches high no mark or scar percievable on his face hands or arms except from the bite of a dog on the right hand and a small scar over the left eye who it appears was emancipated by GRAY EDMUNDS by his last Will & Testament of recording in the County Given under my hand this 7th March 1804.

Reg. No. 2 & cop'd H. Hill

Renewed the 22nd July 1812
do 24th July 1815

=====

Brunswick County to wit This is to Certify that the bearer hereof PHIL a Black man about thirty two years of Age of a black complection about five feet seven or eight Inches high has a Small finger on the little finger on each hand and a small Scar on the left rist who it appears was one of the slaves emancipated by the last Will & Testament of GRAY EDMUNDS dec'd. Given under my hand this 23rd day of April 1804.

Reg. No 3 & cop'd H. Hill CBC

=====

Brunswick County to wit This is to Certify that the bearer hereof BEN a black man about Twenty five years of Age of a yellowish complection about five feet 4 or 5 Inches high has Scar on his forehead & a large scar on the under part of the right arm occasioned by a burn who it appears was one of the slaves emancipated by GRAY EDMUNDS dec'd by his last Will & Testament. Given under my hand this 23rd day of April 18 hundred & four.

Registered No 3 & Cop'd H. Hill CBC
Renewed the 7th August 1810
Renewed 17 Sept. 1813 Teste A. Wesson DC
(Note: Numbered in error by CC ?)

=====

Brunswick County to wit I do hereby Certify that the bearer hereof NED a Black man about Forty two years of Age of a black complection about five feet five or Six Inches high has a small Scar on the right side of his upper lip & another on the right Cheek who it appears was one of the slaves emancipated by BENJA JONES dec'd.by a Deed bearing date the 17th Feby 1801. Given under my hand this 23rd May 1804.

Reg. No. 5 & Cop'd Renewed 23rd July 1807 H. Hill CBC

=====

Brunswick Sc I do hereby Certify that the bearer hereof MOSES is a Black Man about Twenty three years of age about Five Feet 8 or 9 inches high has a Scar near the right eye & another across the left eye Brow and another small one on the upper lip who it appears was one of the slaves emancipated by BENJAMIN JONES dec'd. by Deed bearing date the 17th Feby 1801. Given under my hand the 26 (?) June 1804

Reg. No. 6 & Cop'd H. Hill CBC

=====

Brunswick Sc I do hereby certify that the bearer hereof BERRY is a black man about Thirty three years of Age about five feet Six inches high has a Scar on the under part of the left hand occasioned by a Cut & has two of his upper fore teeth out is one of the slaves emancipated by BENJAMIN JONES as appears by the within copy & certificate given under my hand as clerk of the County Court this 16th day of June 18 hundred & four.

Registered No. 7 & cop'd Herbert Hill CLC

=====

Brunswick Sc I do hereby certify that the bearer hereof ENOS a black man of yellowish complection about Twenty three years of Age Five feet four or five inches high has a scar on the back of the left hand occasioned by a cut has no scar perceivable in the face is one of the slaves emancipated by BENJAMIN JONES dec'd as appears by the certificate of his executor. Given under my hand as clerk of our said County Court this 16th day of June 1804.

Herbert Hill CLC

Registered No. 8 & cop'd
Renewed 24 May 1810

Herbert Hill CBC

=====

Brunswick Co. to wit I do hereby certify that the bearer hereof JACOB otherwise called HUMPHREY a Black man about Forty Five years of age about Five feet Seven inches & a half high has a scar under the right eye & another on the breast & another on the forefinger of the left hand occasioned by a cut it appears is one of the slaves emancipated by the last Will of GRAY EDMUNDS decd. Given under my hand this 23rd day of Augt. 1804 Herbert Hill CLC

Reg. No. 9 & cop'd Renewed 9 Augt.1815

=====

Brunswick Sc I do hereby Certify that the bearer hereof BOB a black man of yellowish complection about twenty seven years of age about Six feet one or two Inches high has no scar perciecable on his hands arms or face but has one on his Left breast who it appears was one of the slaves Emancipated by BENJAMIN JONES dec'd. by Deed bearing date the 17th Feby 1801. Given under my hand this 6th October 1804.

Registered No. 10 & cop'd H. Hill CBC

=====

Brunswick Sc I do hereby Certify that the bearer hereof AMEY a black woman about Thirty Eight or nine years of age about Five feet one Inch high stout made has a scar on her forehead & another between her eyes who it appears was one of the slaves Emancipated by the last Will & Testament of GRAY EDMUNDS Dec'd. Given under my hand this 12th day of December 1804.

Registered No.11 & cop'd Renewed 28 July 1812 H. Hill CLC

=====

Brunswick County Sc   I do hereby certify that the bearer hereof MUMFORT STEWART a black man about 22 years of age about 5 feet 11½ Inches high rather slender made has no scars on his face hands or arms perceivable but has two on his right foot occasioned by the cut of an Ax is free born and has been raised in the County. Given under my hand this 3rd day of October 1805.

Registered No. 12 & cop'd   Herbt. Hill

=====

Brunswick Sc   I do hereby Certify that the bearer hereof ISAAC a black man about twenty four years of Age about five feet eight Inches and a half high a Small Scar on his right hand has had the Smallpox who it appears is one of the slaves emancipated by the last Will & Testament of GRAY EDMUNDS decd. Given under my hand this 24th March 1806.

Registered No. 13 & cop'd   H. Hill CLC
Renewed 14 June 1810   A. Weston DC
Renewed 18th December 1812   W. W. Blanch DC

=====

I do hereby certify that the bearer hereof PLEASANT BURG a black man about Forty one years of age upwards of five feet 10 inches high has no perceivable Scars or marks on his hands arms or face was imancipated by DAVID KIRKLAND on the 1st day of February 1806. Given under my hand this 2nd day of June 1806.

Regd. No. 14 & copy
Renewed June Court 1810 & Examined & Certifyed by the Court
Renewed the 20th July 1813.   A. Wesson DC

=====

I do hereby certify that the bearer hereby FED (commonly called WAGGOONER FED) is a black man who appears to be between forty & forty (sic) years of age about five feet five inche high has no scars or marks on his face hands or arms but has a scar just below the pit of the stomach occasioned from a stab was emancipated by WILLIAM MEREDITH on the 19th day of April 1806.

Regd. No. 15 & cop'd
Renewed & cop'd by the Court June 6th 1811

=====

Brunswick County Sc This is to certify that the bearer hereof JAMES is a black man of yellowish complection appears to be upwards of 40 years of age about five feet five or six Inches high has no per ceivable mark or scar on his face hands or arms has lost the most of his teeth was emancipated by MARY JONES on the 17th day of Feby. 1801 by deed of emancipation. Given etc.

Regd. No. 16 & cop'd 28 Augt. 1806

=====

This is to certify that the bearer hereof ABEDNIGO a black man of a yellowish complection appears to be about thirty six years of age five feet five inches high has no perceiva- ble mark of Scar on his face hands or arms has lost two of his fore- teeth was emancipated by MARY JONES on the 17th of Feby. 1801 by deed of emancipation. Given under my hand etc. 28th Augt. 1806.

No. 17 Regd. & cop'd

=====

This is to certify that the bearer hereof CHARLES a young black man of a yellowish complection about 21 years of age five feet 8½ inches high well made, has a small scar in his forehead was emancipated by BENJ. JONES on the 17th February 1801 by deed of emancipation. Given under my hand this 28th Augt. 1806.

No. 18 Reg. & Cop'd

=====

Brunswick Sc
This is to Certify that the bearer hereof JACK a black man upwards of Fifty years old, has a Scar on the back of his left hand appears to be a Cut, has lost all his teeth except three & they are together about the left eye tooth, was emancipated by the last Will & Testa- ment of WILLIAM HILL dec'd. Given under my hand this 13th September 1806.

Regd. No. 19 & cop'd.

=====

This is to certify that the bearer here ANTHONY SMITH a black man of a yellowish complection about twenty three years of age about five feet six inches high has no mark or scar on his face or hands but has two scars on the under part of the right arm just below the Elbow is the son of a certain MARY SMITH a free woman late of the County of Greensville and was bound by JOHN ROSES overseer of hers (_____) the said County to WILLIAM BROWN as appears by the Indentures of apprenticeship in the possession of the said ANTHONY SMITH. Given under my hand this 27th September 1806.

Reg. No. 20 & Cop'd. H. Hill

=====

This is to Certify that the bearer hereof DAVID JONES is a black man of a Yellowish complection appears to be about Thirty years old five Six Inches high has no perceivable mark or Scar on his face, hands, or arms, was emancipated by BENJAMIN JONES on the 17th Feby. 1801 by Deed of emancipation. Given under my hand this 15th Oct. 1806.

Reg. No 21 & Cop'd.

Brunswick July Court 1814.
The above certificate was compared by the Court with the person of said DAVID & found Correct.

Renewed July 1814 Test. H. Hill CLC

=====

This is to Certify that the bearer hereof NANCY is a black woman of a yellowish Complection is about twenty one years of age about five feet one inch high has no scar on her hands arms or face, has a mold on her left cheek was emancipated by MARY JONES on the 17th Feby 1801 by deed of emancipation. Given under my hand this 15th October 1806.

Registered No 22 & cop'd. H. Hill

=====

This is to certify that the bearer hereof BARNAY STEWART a tall black man, has no particular mark to be distinguished he has a very droning speech when he talks, he is free born as I have always understood & verily believe as he has lived in the county for a number of years. Given under my hand this 2nd Oct. 1806.

Regd. No 23 & cop'd H. Hill CLC

=====

Brunswick Sc
This is to certify that the bearer hereof DANIEL LEWIS a black man is about Fourty-four years of age about five feet ten Inches & a half has no particular scar on his face hands or arms, thin visage is one of the slaves emancipated by OWEN MYRICK by his last Will & Testament of Record in this Court. Given under my hand this 15 November 1806.

Registered No. 24

=====

This is to certify that the bearer hereof ANTHONY a black man Fifty eight years of Age about five feet nine inches high gray hair in his head has no particular mark or scar on his face hands etc the most of his teeth out particularly his upper foreteeth was emancipated by MARY JONES of this County on the 17th Feby. 1801. Given under my hand this 18th November 1806.

Regd. No. 24 (sic) & copd. H. Hill CLC

=====

This is to certify the bearer hereof GEORGE a black man twenty years of age about five feet ten inches & 3/4 high has no particular scar or brand on his face hands or arms he is well make has a large mouth and thick lips was emancipated by MARY JONES of this County on the 17th Feby. 1801. Given under my hand this 19th November 1806.

Regd. No. 25 & cop'd. H. Hill

=====

This is to Certify the bearer hereof TOPSAIL a black man about 21 years of age five feet 10½ inches high of a pleasing countenance has a scar on the right side of the breast occasioned from a burn and on on the right rist just above the thumb no scar on the face was emancipated by MARY JONES of this County on the 17th Feby. 1801. Given under my hand this 19th November 1806.

Reg'd. No. 26 & Cop'd. H. Hill

=====

I do hereby Certify that the bearer hereof is a brown mulatto woman, four feet 10½ Inches high about 32 years of age named AGGY LANTY has no mark or scar on her face hands, arms, was born free and raised in the County of Dinwiddie as appears from the register of JOHN GRAMMER CLK of Pbg Hustings Court which Certificate a copy of this is inserted on. Given under my hand this 22nd day of Dec. 1807.

Reg'd. No 27 & cop'd. H. Hill CBC

=====

I do hereby certify that the bearer hereof WILLIE LAWRENCE a mulatto man abt 21 years of age near 6 feet high is reputed to be the son of NANY LAWRENCE a free woman residing in this county he has no perceivable mark or scar about his face hands or arms on a small scar on the back of his left hand. Given under my hand this 20th March 1808.

Reg'd. No. 28 Herbt. Hill CBC

=====

I do hereby Certify that the bearer hereof WELSHIRE EASTER a Black man about forty eight years of age five feet 6½ Inches high has no scar perceivable on his face hands or arms was emancipated by the last Will & Testament of OWEN MYRICK dec'd. Given under my hand this 21st Sept. 1808.

Reg't No 29 & cop'd. H. Hill CLK

=====

I do hereby Certify that the bearer hereof PETER CAIN a black man about fifty three years of age five feet nine high has a scar on his right wrist, lost several of his teeth was emancipated by the last Will & Testament of OWEN MYRICK dec'd. Given under my hand this 21st day of September 1808.

Reg'd. No. 30 & cop'd Herbert Hill CLK

=====

I do hereby Certify that the bearer hereof LEWIS otherwise called LEWIS ROBERTS a black man of Yellowish complection about Thirty seven years of age five feet 6 Inches high has no scar perceivable on his face hands or arms was emancipated by the last Will & Testament of OWEN MYRICK dec'd. Given under my hand this 21 Sept. 1808.

Registered No 31 & cop'd. Herbert Hill CLC

=====

I do hereby certify that the bearer LEWIS a black man of a yellowish complection about twenty two years old five feet 4½ inches high has no scar or brand on his face or hands one of his foreteeth partly gone was emancipated by BENJAMIN JONES of this County. Given under my hand the 29th day of Jany. 1809.

Registered No 32 & cop'd. H. Hill CLK C

=====

The bearer hereof JOHN a black man about 22 years of age upwards of six feet high has two small scars on the top of the right shoulder was emancipated by MARY JONES of this County. Given under my hand this 29th Jany. 1809.

Reg. 33 H. Hill CLK C

=====

The bearer hereof DANIEL a black man about thirty seven years of age of a yellowish Complection five feet seven or eight inches high, has a scar on the inside of his left leg, and another across the ancle of the same leg, has no scar or mark on his face or arms, appears to be emancipated by EDWARD DROMGOOLE of this County agreeable to the within deed. Examined & allowed by the Court to be correct on the 26th March 1810.

Registered No. 34 Teste Herbert Hill CLK C
Renewed the 25th day of March 1816 Teste H. Hill CLK C

=====

The bearer hereof PHEBY a black woman about fifty years of age no perceivable marks either on the face, head, or hands was emancipated by MARY JONES on the 17th day of February 1801 as appears by deed duly recorded in the county Court of Brunswick & the Court having compared this Certificate with the person of the said PHEOBE allow the same to have been truly made June the 25 day 18 hundred and ten.

Registered No. 35 cop'd Teste Herbert Hill CK. C

=====

The bearer hereof MARY ROBINSON a black girl about Seven years of age a scar on the right arm near the elbow a scar on the left Cheek and an excressence on the left side of the Neck no other perceivable marks about the head face or hands appears to be the daughter of PHOEBE a black woman who was liberated by MARY JONES on the 17th day of February 1801 appears by deed of Emancipation duly Recorded in the County Court of Brunswick & the Court having compared this Certificate with the person of the said MARY ROBINSON allow the same to have been truly made, June the 25 day 1810.

Registered No 36 cop'd Teste Herbert Hill CK. C

=====

Brunswick Sc
I do hereby Certify that the bearer hereof CREASY a black girl of about Twenty years of age, five feet one inch high, stout made & full face has no scar or mark on her face or hands is, as appears by the Certificate of JAMES NOLLY one of the Children of AMEY, a slave formerly emancipated by JOHN SEWARD of this County Certified under my hand this 22nd day of October 1810.

Herbert Hill CBC

Brunswick County October Court 1810
This Certificate was examined by the Court & Certify'd to be correct
Registered No 37 Cop'd Teste H. Hill CBC

=====

Brunswick County to wit
I do hereby certify that the bearer hereof RANDOL a black man about twenty one years old dark Complection tolerably stout made, bow legged, and about five feet three or four inches high no apparent scar or mark on the head face or hands is, as appears by the Certificate of JAMES NOLLY one of the Children of AMEY a woman emancipated by JOHN SEWARD of this County on the 22nd day of June 1789 as appears by the records of the said county of Brunswick. Given under my hand this 23rd day of October 1810.

Herbert Hill CLC

Brunswick County October Court 1810
The above certificate was examined and certified by the Court to be correct.
Registered No. 38 cop'd Teste H. Hill CK C

=====

Brunswick County (to wit)
I do hereby certify that the bearer hereof, ISAAC, a black man of a yellowish Complection about forty two years of age about five feet three inches high, a small scar on the back of the left hand opposite the forefinger & very small scar or mark on the nose between the eyes appears to have been emancipated by JOHN SEWARD agreeable to the withi deed. Given under my hand this 23rd day of October 1810.

Teste Herbert Hill CBC

Brunswick County October Court 1810
The above certificate was examined & compared with the person of the said ISAAC & certified to be correct.

Registered No 39 Cop'd. Teste H. Hill CBC

=====

Teste   Herbert Hill CBC

October 1810
icate was examined by the Court and allowed to be

Cop'd   Teste   H. Hill CBC

of GODFREY ROBINSON, a free black man about Twenty one
x feet high Tolerably slim and dark complected, a
e right side of the upper lip a small round scar on
ppears by the Oath of ALEXANDER WALKER, to be one of
ipated by MARY JONES, now dec'd. of record in the
Brunswick. Given under my hand this 26th day of

l & cop'd   Teste   Herbert Hill CBC

Court February 26, 1841
ption was compared with the person of the said GOD-
by the Court to be correctly taken.
Teste   Herbert Hill CBC

ER OF DOWER SLAVES & C   PAGE 15

---

s in possession of ARMESTEAD GOODWYN and SARAH his
RAH DANCE as Dower Slaves
aged 50. STEPHEN 45. JOE 25. TONY 19. DAVY 6. GILLAM

aged 50. USSA 26. AMY 14. LUCY 12. PHEBE 2.

unswick County Court Clerks office the __dayof___.
Teste   Herbert Hill CBC

ws now my possession belonging to the Estate of
K dec'd with thare sex's & ages annext to thare names
805 Herbert Edwards.

40 yrs. old. LEWIS 27. HARY 21 JHACOB 9. STERLING
s. SAMUEL 5. 6 mos. MOSES 3. 1 mo. CHARY 4, 3 m.
M 5 mos.
CE 58 years. LUCY 37. LIDDAH 35. SARY 27. LUCY 25
AH 11. RHODY 10. 7 mos. BOLING 8-8 mos. HANAH 5.6 mos.

ESBELL 3. 6 mos. PATIENCE 1. 3 mos. MASON 7 months.

Returned into Brunswick County Court Clerks office the 23rd day of September 1805

Teste Herbert Hill CBC

=====

A list of Negroes belonging to me during life as the widow of BRITAIN REBLES.

BOB 1. ROBEN 2. JACK 3. JIM___. HUBBARD 4. TOM 5. WILL 6. NATHAN 7. TURNER 8. NAN 9. NELL 10. LUCY 11. ELIZA 12. NANCY 13. ROANNY 14. MACKY 15. CHERRY 16. FRANCIS 17.

Returned into Brunswick County Court Clerk's Office the (_____) day of March 1809. Teste Herbert Hill CBC

One Negro fellow named JAMES aged about 25 or six years held for the life of the wife of MOSES CALLEHAM who was the widow of (_________) CALLEHAM.

James Rawlings
April 1st 1809

Returned into Brunswick County Court Clerks office the (______) day of (______) 1809.

Teste Herbert Hill CBC

REGISTER OF DOWER SLAVES & C Continued

List of Dower Slave held by BARRINGTON AVERY in right of his wife in Est. of ABM. MITCHELL.

ABRAM born June the 26, 1803. NANCY born Sept. 21st 1806. JACK born August the 21st. 1810.

Returned into Brunswick County Court Clerks Office the 22nd day of October 1810.

Teste Herbert Hill CBC

A list of Negroes borne in the possession of BARRINGTON AVERY held by by him durring life by virtue of his intermarriage with REBECCA MITCH widow of ABRAHAM MITCHELL dec'd. borne December 23rd 1815. ANNALIZA daughter of PHILLIS borne January 12th 1815.

Returned into Brunswick County Court Clerks Office March 23rd 1815.
Teste Herbert Hill CBC

=====

Brunswick Sc
I do hereby certify that the bearer hereof a black man named NAT MOSS a black man of a dark complection about twenty two years of age five feet nine inches High, has a scar on the inside of the right arm just below the Elbow and another on the back of his left hand was free born as appears by the Oath of TILMAN AVERY in court. Given under my hand this 28th day of May 1811.

Registered No. 42 Herbert Hill CBC

1811 May 28th Examined by the Court & found to be Correct.
Teste Herbert Hill CBC

=====

Brunswick Sc
I do hereby Certify that the bearer hereof MINGO a black man about 33 years dark Complexion about five feet six inches high, a small scar on the back part of the left Cheek one on the breast and one on the left arm above the Elbow is one of the Negros Emancipated by the last Will and Testament of WILLIAM WALKER dec'd. of record in the County Court of Brunswick aforesaid, as appears by the Oath of ____ Rec'd. 1/6 pd. in Court. Given under my hand this 23rd day of September 1811.

Registered No. 43

=====

Brunswick Sc
This is to Certify that the bearer hereof MOSES a black man about 6 feet high 28 or 9 years old has a scar under the right eye and on the right side of his breast was emancipated by PETER ROBINSON exor of BENJA JONES who was exor of WILLIAM WALKER as will appear by a copy of the deed of Emancipation which the copy of this register is on. Given under my hand this 23rd Sept. 1811.
Registered No. 44 H. Hill

13th Sept. Ct. examined by the Court & found correct.
Teste H. Hill

=====

Brunswick Sc
I do hereby certify that the bearer hereof CHARLES a black man of a dark complection five feet 2 or 3 inches high about 21 years of age has no perceivable mark or scar on his face hands or arms is one of the slaves emancipated by JNO SEWARD as appears by a copy of the Deed on which the copy of this Registered is on. Given under my hand this 23rd Sept. 1811.

BK Super Ct. 1811 Exd. by the Court & found correct.
Registered No. 45 Teste H. Hill CBC

=====

Brunswick Sc
I do hereby that the bearer hereof BUCK BLANTON a mulatto man five feet five inches high about 21 years of age, has a scar on the right side of his face near the Corner of his mouth two upper teeth inside of his mouth a scar on the right arm below the Elbow was free born. Given under my hand this 25th day of May 1812.

Registered No. 46 Teste H. Hill CK

=====

A list of Slaves in the possession of LUCY MALONE widow of GEORGE MALONE dec'd.

ABSALOM	aged 50	ISHAM	aged 45
JERRY	" 39	LUCY	" 45
DESON	" 16	TOM	" 12

Brunswick County Court May 25th 1812
This list of the ages & sexes of the slaves held by LUCY MALONE was returned into Court & ordered to be recorded.

Teste Herbert Hill CBC

=====

Brunswick County Sc
I do hereby Certify that the bearer hereof BILLY a black man about twenty one or twenty two years of age is the son of MARIA a black woman Emancipated by HENRY MERRITT of this County he is about five three or four Inches has two Small Scars on the inside of the right arm & two on the back of the right hand. Given under my hand this 24th day of August 1812.

Registered No. 47

Bunswick County August Court 1812
The above Certificate Examined & found Correct.
Renewed 28 August 1815 A copy Teste H. Hill CBC

=====

Brunswick County Sc
I do hereby Certify that the bearer hereof EDMUND MATTHEWS a free man of a yellow Complexion about twenty two or twenty three years of age about five feet ten or eleven inches high has a Small Scar on the inside of his left rist & a few Small ones on each arm three Jaw teeth out on the left Side & no other scar on his face perceivably Who it appears was freeborn. Given under my hand this 24th day of August 1812.

Registered No. 48 Herbert Hill CBC

=====

Brunswick Sc
I do hereby Certify that the bearer hereof ISAAC is a black man by the name of ISAAC aged twenty nine years has an impedemant in his Speech five feet five eight inches & a half high a scar on the right Elbow one on the top of the left wrist one on the nuckle of the forefinger of the left hand one over the right eye one under the throat appears to be one of the Slaves Emancipated by the last Will & Testament of WILLIAM WALKER dec'd late of this County. Given under my hand this 27th day of October 1812.

H. Hill CBC

Brunswick County October Court 1812. The above Certificate examined by the Court & found Correct. A copy Teste H. Hill CBC
Regist. 49 Teste David Meade

=====

Brunswick Sc
I do hereby Certify that the bearer hereof JACK ROBERTS a black man of a yellow Complexion about thirty one years of age about five feet seven or eight Inches high one small Scar a little above the elbow of the right arm no other Scar or mark perceivable who it appears was emancipated by the last Will & Testament of OWEN MYRICK dec'd. Given under my hand this 25th day of January 1813.

Teste Herbert Hill CBC

Brunswick County Court January 25th 1813
The abve certificate was examined by the Court and found to be correct.

Registered No. 50 Teste Herbert Hill CBC

=====

Brunswick Sc
I do hereby Certify that the bearer hereof ANTHONY is a black man about Twenty four or five years of age five feet Six or Seven Inches high 2 small scars over the eyes a scar above the Wrist of the left arm another Small one on the right arm above the Wrist and another one under the wrist of the same arm no other scar or mark perceivable who it appears was emancipated by the last Will & Testament of OWEN MYRICK dec'd. Given under my hand this 25th day of Feby. 1813.

Teste Herbert Hill

Brunswick County Court February 23rd 1813
The above Certificate was Examined by the Court and found to be Correct.
WM EDWD BRODNAX a Copy
(Note: No register number given. Should be 51.)
Renewed 30th October Teste H. Hill CBC

=====

Brunswick Sc
I do hereby Certify that the bearer hereof SAMUEL JONES HERCULAS a black man of a yellow complection twenty one years of age about five feet 10 inches high has a scar on the left eye brow another between the left eye & ear and another on the under part of the right arm near the elbow was emancipated by BENJAMIN JONES late of this County by a deed of Emancipation. Given under my hand this 25th day of May 1813

Registered No. 52 Herbert Hill CBC

=====

Brunswick County Sc
I do hereby Certify that the bearer hereof THOMAS LAWRENCE a mulatto man about twenty one years of age five feet ten inches high of a bright complection has no mark or scar on his face, hands or arms, was born free in this county as appears by the certificate of JOHN ELLIOTT. Given under my hand this 25th day of May 1813.

Registered No. 53 Herbert Hill CBC

Brunswick County Court May 25 1813
Exd by the Court & found correct
Teste JS Pritchett Teste H. Hill CBC

=====

Brunswick Sc
I do hereby certify that the bearer hereof SUSANA WARD Mulatto woman aged twenty three years about five feet six inches high has a scar over the left eye brow was emancipated by MICHAEL MALONE of the County of Sussex as appears by an attested copy of his will. Given under my hand this 24th day of Augt. 1813.

Registered No. 53 (Sic) H. Hill CBC

=====

Brunswick Sc
I do hereby Certify that the bearer hereof PATTY GRAIN a black woman of a yellow complection about twenty eight or nine years of age five feet two inches high has a Scar about the middle of the forehead and another over the right eyebrow was one of the slaves emancipated by OWEN MYRICK late of this county by his last Will & Testament of record in this county. Given under my hand this ___ day of 1813.

Registered No. 55

=====

Brunswick County Sc
I do hereby certify that the bearer hereof BRITAIN GRAIN a black man five feet 3 Inches & better high about thirty one years of age has a scar across the forehead rather over the left eyebrow is one of the slaves emancipated by the last Will & Testament of OWEN MYRICK dec'd of record in this County Court. Given under my hand this 24th day of 1813.

Registered No. 56 Herbert Hill

Brunswick County Court January 25th 1813
The above Certificate was examined by the Court and found to be correct.
Registered No. 51 & copd. Teste H. Hill CBC

=====

Brunswick Sc
I do hereby Certify that the bearer hereof DESSY a black woman about forty five years of age five feet two or three Inches high has several Scars on the right arm and one on the left no Scar on the face is one of the slaves emancipated by HENRY MOSS late of the County of Sussex as appears from the evidence of ____ . Given under my hand this 26th day of May 1813.

Registered No. 54 (sic) & copd. Herbert Hill CBC

Brunswick County Court 1813
This Certificate was examined by the Court and found to be Correct.
Teste Herbert Hill CBC

=====

Brunswick Sc
I do hereby certify that the bearer LUCY alias LUCY WALKER a black woman about 5 feet 3 or 4 inches high Twenty six years of age has several small marks or scars on her arms no mark on the face thick lips and has holes in her ears made for the purpose of wearing ear rings is one of the slaves emancipated by PETER ROBINSON's exor of WM. WALKER dec'd by virtue of a decree in the high Court of chancery held at Richmond. Given under my hand this 23rd day of Augt. 1813

Registered No. 57 Teste H. Hill

Brunswick County Augt. 23rd 1813
Exd & found Correct. Teste H. Hill CBC

=====

Brunswick County Sc
I do hereby Certify that the bearer JAMES CHANCE (alias JAMES DABNEY) a mulatto man about forty five years of age five six & a Quarter inches high, has no scar or mark on his face hands or arms was born free as appears by the certificate of JOHN GOODRUM of Greensville and EDWD PEGRAM of Dinwiddie. Given under my hand this 27th September 1813.

Registered No. 58 Herbert Hill C B C

Brunswick County Septmber Court 1813
The above Certificate was examined by the Court and found to be corr
A copy Teste

=====

Brunswick County Sc
I do hereby Certify that the bearer hereof, JOHN STEWART a black of a yellow complexion five feet nine or ten inches high about Twenty five or six years old has two Scars on above the other in the forehead no other Scar or mark on the face hands or arms of any note or size has a stoppage in his Speech when spoken to, his hair rather inclined to be Straight was freeborn in this county giver under my hand this 23rd day November 1813

Registered No. 59 & copd Teste Herbert Hill C B C

Brunswick County November Court 1813
The above Certificate was examined by the Court & found Correct.
Teste Jno Wyche A copy Teste H. Hill C B C

=====

Jno Stewarts No 60 Registered at the end of processioning for 1813

=====

I do hereby Certify that the bearer hereof ISAAC MOSS a man of Colou about twenty one years old five feet 7½ Inches high has a long scar on the left wrist three small ones on the ball of the same hand of a dark complexion was born free as appears by the evidence of _____ in Court. Given under my hand this 28th day of March 1814

Registered No. 61 Copd
The above description compared with the person of said ISAAC MOSS & found correct at March Court 1814 Teste H. Hill CLK

=====

y February Court 1814
ficate was compared with the person of said FRANKEY
to be Correct. Teste H. Hill CBC

tify that the bearer hereof ABRAM ROBERTS a man of
e dark Complexion, supposed to be about Forty years
t 9½ Inches, a scar on the right cheek and another on
he left hand his head turning grey, is also a scar
rather over the left eyes one of the person eman-
last Will and Testament of OWEN MYRICK dec'd (of record
ourt of Brunswick) as appears from the evidence of

63 & copd.

ourt 1814
ficate was compared by the Court with the person of
RTS & found correct.
Teste H. Hill C B C

y Sc
tify that the bearer hereof NED JONES HERCULAUS a free
twenty one or two years five feet five or six inches
en scar (apparently three) adjoining under the rite
e 1 small scar on the arm of the right hand with the
he fourth finger of the right hand has been nearly
appears was emancipated by the last Will & Testament
ES, dec'd given under my hand this 28th day of March

4 & copd. Teste Herbert Hill C B C

y Court March 1815
e was examined by the Court and compared with the
aid NED JONES HERCULAUS & found to be Correct.
A copy Teste Herbert Hill C B C

y the last Will and Testament of WILLIAM WALKER
ler my hand this 23rd day of August 1815

Teste Herbert Hill C B C

Court August 23rd 1813 (sic). Examined by the Court
.

Teste Herbert Hill C B C

ify that the bearer hereof JACOB (otherwise called
nan of Colour of a dark complexion Twenty one years
e feet three inches high has a scar on the left cheak
of the mouth a scar on the middle finger of the right
ions it to be crooked who it appears is the son of
nancipated by HENRY MERRITT of this County. Given
is 29th day of August 1815.

5 Herbert Hill C B C

Court August 29, 1815
icate was examined by the Court and compared with the
id JACOB and found correct.

A copy Teste H. Hill C B C

Sc
ereby Certify that the bearer hereof LUKE MATTHEWS a
f a yellow complexion, about five feet nine inches
or three years old has a scar nearly midway between
on the thumb of the left arm near and adjoining the
he joint of the thumb with the hand of the same arm
t the joint of the hand with the wrist of the same
other noted scars or marks perceivable. Given under
h day of August 1815.

7 Herbert Hill C B C

Court August 29th 1815
icate was examined by the Court and compared with the
id MATTHEWS & found correct.

Teste Herbert Hill C B C

Brunswick County Sc

I do hereby that the bearer hereof ROBERT CROOK a free man of Colour of a yellow complexion, about six feet high about twenty years of age has no scars or marks perceivable except a small one a little back of the first joint of the forefinger and left hand who it appears is the son of BETTY CROOK who was emancipated by JOSEPH CROOK formerly of this County. Given under my hand this 25th day of December 1815.

Registered No. 68 Teste Herbert Hill C B C

Brunswick County January Court 1816
The above Certificate was examined by the Court and Compared with the person of the said CROOK & found Correct.
Teste Teste Herbert Hill C B C
John Wyche JP.

=====

Brunswick County Sc

I do hereby Certify that the bearer hereof ANDREW JONES HERCULAS about Twenty one years of age five feet five or Six inches of a yellow complexion has a small scar on the first finger near the first Joint thereof and another near the Joint of the thumb the first Joint thereof of the left hand. No other scars or marks perceivable on his face hands or arms who it appears by the evidence of WILLIAM YATES was emancipated by BENJAMIN JONES, formerly of this County. Given under my hand this 25th March 1815.

Registered No. 69 & copy'd. Herbert Hill C B C

Brunswick County Court March 25th 1816
The above certificate was examined with the person of the said HERCULAS & found correct.
Teste Herbert Hill C B C

=====

Brunswick Sc

I do hereby certify that the bearer hereof PLEASANT BURG a free black man about fifty years of age upwards of five feet, ten inches high has no perceivable mark scar on his head face or hands was emancipated by DAVID KIRKLAND on the first of February 1806 as will appear by deed of emancipation of that date. Given under my hand this 29th day of August 1816.

Registered No. 70 & copd H. Hill C B C

Brunswick County Court August term 1816
This Certificate was examined by the Court with the person of said PLEASANT BURG & found Correct. Given under my hand this 27 August 1816.
Teste W.W. Blanch D C

=====

Brunswick County Sc
I do hereby Certify that the bearer hereof MARTHA (alias MARTHA JONE) a free woman of Colour rather of a Yellow complexion Twenty one or two Years of Age five feet four or five Inches high has two scars on the left Arm one a little below the Joint of the arm the other between three or four Inches lower down more inside of the arm one black speck opposite the joint of the Thumb on the left hand one scar between the second & third joint of the middle finger and left hand two small ones on the back of the right hand one other scar a little to the right of her forehead one other just under lower lip who it appears was mancipated by MARY JONES formerly of this County. Given under my hand this day of Twenty Sixth August 1816.

Registered No. 71 H. Hill C B C

Brunswick County Court August 26th 1816
This Above Certificate was examined by the Court with the person of said MARTHA JONES and found correct.
Teste A copy Teste H. Hill C B C

=====

Brunswick Sc
I do hereby Certify that the bearer hereof JOHN CANE a free black man Twenty one or two years old five feet nine Inches high one rising Scar on the tip of the elbow of the left hand Seven other Scars on said arm another rising scar on the tip of the elbow of the right arm six other scars on the same arm four other scars on & around the sc Joint of right hand one scar on the 2nd joint of forefinger of the left hand who it appears was free born by the information WILLIAM P. WALKER. Given under my hand this 28th Octr. 1816.
Countersigned
JOHN WYCHE Teste Herbert Hill C B C

Registered No. 72 & Copd

Brunswick County Court October term 1816
The within Certificate was compared by the Court with the person of the said CANE and found Correct.
Teste Herbert Hill C B C

=====

Brunswick Sc

I do hereby certify that the bearer hereof JACOB MERRETT a free black man about twenty two years of age of a dark complexion one scar a little leftward of the left corner of the mouth and appearance of the middle finger of the right hand being cut off but united ? five feet four inches high who it appears was emancipated by HENRY MERRETT of this county as appears by the evidence of WILLIAM M DUGGAR. Given under my hand this 29th day of October 1816.

Registered No. 73 & Copd.
Countersigned
Jno. Wyche Teste Herbert Hill C B C

Brunswick County Court October term 1816
This certificate was compared by the person of the said JACOB MERRITT and found correct.
Teste Herbert Hill C B C

=====

Brunswick Sc

I do hereby certify that the bearer hereof JEREMIAH LEWIS a free man of colour about Twenty four or five years of age five feet eight inches high of a dark complexion has a scar a little to the right of the right eye another over the right eye as well as several small one's interspersed on his hand who it appears was one of the slaves emancepated by OWEN M MYRICK formerly of this County by the evidence of WILLIAM WILKINSON. Given under my hand this 27th day of January 1817.
Registered No. 74 & Copd Teste R. Turnbull C B C

Brunswick County Court January 27th 1817
This Certificate was examined by the Court and ordered to be Certified.
Teste R. Turnbull C B C

=====

Brunswick County Sc

I do hereby certify that the bearer hereof HERBERT MOSS a free black man Twenty one or two years old five feet Six inches high has a Scar occasioned by a Scald under the arm of & near the wrist of his left hand, a mold on the wrist of the left hand near the joint of the thumb who it appears was emancipated by HENRY MOSS. Given under my hand this 24 March 1817.

Registered No. 75 Copd R. Turnbull

Brunswick County Court March term 1817
The above certificate was examined by the Court with the person of the said MOSS & found correct.
Teste Philip Pryor Teste R. Turnbull C B C

=====

Brunswick County Sc
I do hereby certify that the bearer hereof HANNAH WALKER a free woman of Colour rather light complexion five feet six & half inches high aged about Twenty six years has a large Scar on the left Side of the neck another on the tip of elbow of the right hand & the others between the wrist & Elbow who it appears by the evidence of HOWELL SIMMS was emancipated by the last Will & Testament of WILLIAM WALKER decd. Given under my hand this 26th day of May 1817

Teste R. Turnbull CBC

John Wyche J P
Registered No. 76 & Cop'd.
Brunswick County Court May Term 1817
The above Certificate was examined by the Court & found Correct.
A copy R. Turnbull C B C

=====

Brunswick County Sc
I do hereby Certify that the bearer hereof SUCKEY WALKER a free woman of Colour dark complexion about five feet four or five Inches high has Several Scars on the arm of the right hand Elbow aged forty seven years, who it appears by the evidence of HOWELL SIMMS was emancipated by the last Will & Testament of WILLIAM WALKER dec'd. Given under my hand this 27 day of May 1817
Teste
Jno. Wyche J P R. Turnbull C B C
Registered No. 77 & Copd

Brunswick County Court May Term 1817
The above Certificate was compared by the Court & found Correct.
A copy R. Turnbull C B C

=====

Brunswick Sc
I do hereby Certify that the bearer herof CHARLES WALKER a free man of Colour Twenty four years old five feet five inches high, has two scars or marks on his left arm perceivable rather light complexion, who it appears by the evidence of HOWELL SIMMS was emancipated by WILLIAM WALKER dec'd. formerly of this County. Given unde my hand this 27th day of May 1817.

Teste John Wyche J P R. Turnbull C B C
Registered No. 78 Copd

Brunswick County Court May Term 1817
The above Certificate was examined by the Court & found Correct.
Teste R. Turnbull

=====

Brunswick Sc
I do hereby certify that the bearer hereof VINEY otherwise VINEY SEWARD a free woman of color about Twenty years of age four feet ten inches high of a yellow complexion has a scar on the nail (which was occasioned by cutting the same), on the fourth finger of the left hand no other perceivable, who it appears was emancipated by JOHN SEWARD of this county. Given under my hand this 22nd day of Septem 1817.
Registered No. 79 R. Turnbull C B C

Brunswick County Court September term 1817
The above Certificate was examined & found Correct.
Countersigned Thos. Parham J P Teste R. Turnbull C B C

=====

Brunswick County Sc
I do hereby Certify that the bearer hereof BETTY WALKER a free woman of Colour about fifteen or sixteen years old rather light complexion has a scar on the right side of the neck near the Jaw five feet four inches high who it appears by the evidence of JESSE KENNEDY was emancipated by the last will & testament of WILLIAM WALKER decd. formerly of this county. Given under my hand this 27th day of October 1817.

Registered No. 80 & Cop'd. R. Turnbull C C

Brunswick County Court October 27 1817
This Certificate was compared by the Court & found Correct.
Teste R. Turnbull C C

=====

Brunswick County Sc
I do hereby Certify that the bearer hereof POLLY WALKER a free woman of Colour about eighteen years old light complexion has two Scars on the Breast near the neck another Scar on the back right wrist and another just above the same wrist five feet Six Inches high who it appears by the evidence of JESSE KENNEDY was emancipated by the last Will & Testament of WILLIAM WALKER decd formerly of this county. Given under my hand this 27 day of October 1817.

Register No. 81 Cop'd R. Turnbull

Brunswick County Court October 27th 1817
This Certificate was examined by the Court and found Correct.
Teste R. Turnbull CBC

=====

Brunswick County Sc

I do hereby certify that the bearer hereof CLARISSA WALKER a free woman of colour about Twenty one years old, dark complection, the thumb & forefinger of the right hand much injured by a burn Five feet & one half inch high who it appeared by the evidence of _____ was emancipated by the last Will & Testament of WILLIAM WALKER dec'd of this county. Given under my hand this 22nd June 1818

Registered No. 82 Cop'd R. Turnbull C B C
This Certificate was examined in Court & found correct.
Teste R. Turnbull C B C

=====

Brunswick County to wit:

I do hereby certify that the bearer hereof BOB a black man about twenty nine years old five feet Ten Inches high has a mole on the breast no other mark or scar obtained his freedom in the Superior Court of Brunswick by a suit in said Court against the executors of HERBERT HILL dec'd Given under my hand this 25th day of June 1818.

R. Turnbull C B C

Brunswick County Court June term 1818
The above certificate was examined & compared with the person of the said BOB & found to be correct.
Js. Pritchett JP
Registered No. 83 Cop'd Teste R. Turnbull C B C

=====

Brunswick County to wit

I do hereby certify that the bearer hereof STEPHEN a black man about thirty five years of age five feet four Inches & an half high a scar over the left eye five flesh Moles on the breast and seven Moles on the back & shoulder & a Mould under the left year Obtained his freedom in the Superior Court of Brunswick by a suit in said Court against the executors of HERBERT HILL dec'd. Given under my hand this 23rd day of June 1818.

R. Turnbull C B C

Brunswick County Court June Term 1818
The above certificate was examined and compared with the person of the said STEPHEN & certified to be correct.
J. Pritchett JP
Registered No. 84 Cop'd. Teste R. Turnbull C B C

=====

Brunswick County to wit
I do certify that the bearer hereof CATO a man of Colour about forty two years of age five feet six & a half Inches high light complexion, has a mole under the left nostril, was emancipated by Deed from RICHARD M CUNNINGHAM & was allowed to remain in this state by the County Court of Brunswick. Given under my hand this 23rd Aug. 1818.

R. Turnbull C B C

Brunswick County Court August Term 1818
The above Certificate was examined & Compared with the person of the said CATO & Certified to be Correct.
Registered No. 85 & Cop'd

=====

Brunswick County Sc
I do Certify that the bearer hereof PETER (who calls himself PETER BOLLING) a free man of Colour about Forty two years old, dark complection has a large Scar on the left arm above the elbow, occasioned by a burn & another Scar on the same arm below the Elbow five feet 6 Inches & 3/4 high, who it appears was emancipated by deed from HENRY MERRITT of Record in this court. Given under my hand this 23rd August 1818.

R. Turnbull C B C

Brunswick County Court August Term 1818
The above Certificate was examined & compared with the person of the said PETER & found Correct.
Registered No. 86 & Cop'd. A copy Teste R. Turnbull C B C

=====

Brunswick County to wit
I do Certify that the bearer hereof ROBERT a free man of Color about Fifty years of age, dark complection the little finger on the left hand crooked, Five feet nine Inches high, who it appears was emancipated by the last Will & Testament of OWEN MYRICK dec'd. of Record in this suit. Given under my hand this 25th day of August 1818.

R. Turnbull C B C

Brunswick County August Term 1818
The above Certificate was examined & compared with the person of the said ROBERT & found correct.
Registered No.87 & cop'd.

=====

Brunswick County to wit
I do hereby certify that the bearer hereof JOHN STEWART a free man of Colour of a yellow complexion five feet nine Inches high about twenty eight or nine years old has two Scars one above the other in the forehead, no other Scar or mark on the face hands or arms has an impediment in his speech, his hair rather inclined to be straight, was free born in this County. Given under my hand this 23rd November 1818.

R. Turnbull C B C

Brunswick County Court November Term 1818
The above certificate was examined by the court and found to be correct.
Teste Jno. H Chapman A Copy R. Turnbull
Registered No. 88

=====

Brunswick County to wit
I do Certify that the bearer hereof PEGGY a free Woman of Colour dark complexion eighteen years old Five feet high, no marks perceivable appears was emancipated by the last Will & Testament of GRAY EDMUNDS dec'd of Record in this Court. Given under my hand this 24th Nov. 1818.

R. Turnbull

The above Certificate was examined & compared with the person of the said PEGGY & found Correct.
Teste
Registered No. 89

=====

Brunswick County to wit
I do certify that the bearer hereof CHARLES MERRITT a man of dark complexion Thirty seven years old Five feet nine one quarter Inches high a scar on the right wrist & one on the breast was emancipated by HENRY MERRITT by deed of Record in this Court. Given under my hand this 22nd February 1819.

Jas. Powell R. Turnbull C B C

The above certificate was examined & compared with the person of the said CHARLES MERRITT found correct.
Teste Registered No. 90

=====

Brunswick County to wit

I do hereby Certify that the bearer hereof POLLY PRITCHETT a Woman of light Complexion about 29 years of age Five feet 4¼ Inches high has a Scar on the left cheek was emancipated by BENJ. JONES by Deed of Record in this Office. Given under my hand this 25th May 18 1819

R. Turnbull C B C

The above Certificate was examined & compared with the person of POLLY PRITCHETT & found correct.
Registered No. 91

=====

Brunswick County to wit

I do hereby Certify that the bearer hereof JUDITH a woman of light complexion about 21 years of age Five feet high has a lengthy scar on the left Arm occasioned by a Cut was emancipated by BENJA JONES by Deed of Record in this Office. Given under my hand this 25th May 1819

R. Turnbull C B C

The above Certificate was examined & Compared with the person of the said JUDITH & found correct.
Registered No. 92

=====

Brunswick County to wit

I do certify that the bearer hereof CATY a woman about Forty years of age, light complexion Five feet one & a half Inches high has a scar on her left arm occasioned by a cut, recovered her freedom in Brunswick Superior Court at September term 1819 of JOHN WYCHE. Given under my hand this 27th day of September 1819.

Jas. Powell R. Turnbull C B C

Brunswick County Court September 27th 1819
The above Certificate was examined & compared with the person of the said CATY & found correct.
Registered No. 93 Teste R. Turnbull C B C

=====

Brunswick County to wit

I do hereby certify that the bearer hereof DILCEY a black woman about fifty one years of age five feet two or three inches high has several scars on the right arm and one on the left no scar in the face is one of the slaves emancipated by HENRY MOSS late of the County of Sussex as appears from the evidence of WILLIAM GEE. Given unde my hand this 25th October 1819

Registered No. 94 R. Turnbull C B C

Brunswick County October Court 1819
The above certificate was compared with the person of the said DILCY and found to be correct.

Teste R. Turnbull C C

=====

Brunswick County Sc

I do hereby certify that the bearer hereof FED (commonly called WAGGONNER FED) is a black man who appears to be fifty five years of age and about five feet five Inches high has no scar or mark on his face hands, or arms, but has a scar just below the pit of the Stomach occasioned from a stab was emancipated by WILLIAM MEREDITH on the nineteenth day of April eighteen hundred & six.
No. 95
Brunswick County Court March 25th 1820
This Certificate was examined by the Court with the person of the said FED and found Correct.

=====

Brunswick County to wit

I do hereby certify that the bearer hereof BETSY MERRITT a free woman twenty two years of age five feet four and ½ inches high has a scar on the right side of the forehead occasioned by a cut with an axe, and was emancipated by HENRY MERRITT of this county as appears by the evidence of THOMAS LANIER which deed of emancipation is on record in this court. Given under my hand this 28th day of March 1820.

No. 96
J. Pritchett JP

Brunswick County Court 28th March 1820
The above certificate was compared with the person of the said BETSEY MERRITT & found correct.

R. Turnbull

=====

Brunswick County to wit

I do hereby certify that the bearer hereof FRANKEY MERRITT aged twenty seven years five feet nine Inches high, has a scar on the right side of the neck and was emancipated by HENRY MERRITT of this county as appears by the evidence of THOMAS LANIER. Given under my hand this 28th day of March 1820.

No. 97
J. Pritchett JP

Brunswick County Court 28th March 1820
The above certificate was compared with the person of the said FRANKEY MERRITT and found correct.

=====

Brunswick County to wit

I do hereby certify that FRANK alias, FRANK LAWRENCE, about twenty eight years of age five feet five & ¼ Inches high and of a yellow complexion has no marks or scars perceivable and by occupation a carpenter who it appears by the evidence of THOMAS LANIER was born free. Given under my hand this 28th day March 1820.

No. 98

Brunswick County Court March 28th 1820
The above certificate was compared with the person of the said FRANK LAWRENCE & found correct.

=====

Brunswick County to wit

I do hereby certify that GODFREY BROWN a free man of colour, aged fifty two years old about five feet 10½ Inches high yellow complexion has two scars on his left arm near the elbow, carries the marks of the small pox on the face, and was emancipated by JOHN T BOWDOIN, as will appear by reference to the deed of emancipation duly recorded in the County Court aforesaid. Given under my hand this 28th day of March 1820.

Registered No. 99

Brunswick County Court February 1820
The above certificate was compared by the court with the person of said GODFREY BROWN & found correct.

(No signature)

=====

Brunswick County to wit

I do hereby certify that the bearer hereof GODFREY OWEN a free man of colour between twenty two and twenty three years of age black complexion six feet & ½ Inch high has no scar or mark perceivable and by occupation a ditcher, who was free born as appears from the evidence of _____ . Given under my hand 24th day of May 1820.

Register No. 100
C. Cordle JP Teste R Turnbull C B C

Brunswick County Court 25th May 1820
The above Certificate was compared with the person of the said GODFREY OWEN & found correct.

Teste R Turnbull C B C

=====

Brunswick County to wit

I do hereby certify that the bearer hereof BENN OWEN a free man of colour about twenty one years of age five feet nine Inches high has a scar on the temple of the right side of the head and another just above the ancle of the left leg, has no other perceivable mark or scar and was born free. Given under my hand this 27th day of May 1820.

R Turnbull C C

Registered No. 101
John B Rice, JP

Brunswick County Court May the 27th 1820
The above certificate was compared with the person of the said BEN OWEN and found correct.

===== Teste R Turnbull C C

START of BOOK II

Brunswick County to wit

I do hereby certify that the bearer hereof THOMAS B. THOMAS a free man of a black complexion about thirty one years of age five feet nine inches high, has no marks or scars perceivable, and by occupation a Black Smith, who was emancipated by the last Will and Testament of OWEN MYRICK deceased, duly recorded in the County Court of Brunswick. Given under my hand this 29th day of August 1820.

Registered No. 102

Brunswick County Court 29th August 1820

The above certificate was compared with the person of the said THOMAS B. THOMAS and found to be correct.

Teste Turnbull CBC

=====

Brunswick County to wit

I do hereby certify that the bearer of DANIEL MERRITT a free man of a black complexion, about twenty two or twenty three years of age, five feet six Inches high, hat but one mark perceivable which is on the outside between the ancle, and knee of the left leg and was free born as appears from the evidence of WILLIAM M.DUGGER. Given under my hand this 29th day of August 1820.

Registered No. 103

Brunswick County August 29th 1820

The above certificate was compared with the person of the said DANIEL MERRITT and found to be correct.

Teste R Turnbull CBC

=====

Brunswick County to wit

I do hereby certify that the bearer hereof SUCKEY GRAIN a free woman of a yellow complection, about nineteen years old, five feet one & an half inch high, has no scars or marks about her face hands or arms except one on the thumb of the right hand which appears to have been caused by a rising, and which said Woman was born free as appears from the evidence of BENJAMIN PHIPPS. Given under my hand this 25th day of September 1820.

Register No. 104

Brunswick County Court September 25th 1820

The above Certificate was compared with the person of the said SUCKEY GRAIN and found to be correct.

Teste R Turnbull CBC

=====

Brunswick County to wit

I do hereby certify that the bearer hereof STEPHEN LEWIS a free man of black complection about twenty two or twenty three years of Age Six feet one inch high, has one scar perceivable which is on the elbow of the right arm occasioned by a burn, and was free born as appears from the evidence of WM PALMER & RICHARD FLETCHER. As witness my hand this 25th of September 1820.

Register No. 105

Brunswick County Court September 25th 1820

The above certificate was compared with the person of the said STEPHEN LEWIS and found to be correct.

Teste R Turnbull CBC

=====

Brunswick County to wit

I do hereby certify that the bearer hereof ANTHONY a black man, about twenty seven or eight years of age five feet six or seven Inches high two small scars over the eyes, a scar above the wrist of the left arm, another small one on the right arm above the wrist and another one inside of the wrist of the same arm, no other scar or mark perceivable, who it appears was emancipated by the last Will and Testament of OWEN MYRICK dec'd. Given under my hand this 25th September 1820.

Register No. 106

Green Hill J. Peace

Brunswick County October Court 1820

The above certificate was Compared with the person of the said ANTHONY and found to be correct.

Teste R Turnbull CBC

=====

Brunswick County S ct

I do hereby certify that the bearer hereof JINCEY LANTY a free woman of a black complexion about nineteen years old, four feet one & ½ Inch high, has no scars or marks on her face, head or arms perceivable, and was free born as appears from the evidence of ____. Given under my hand this 23rd October one thousand eight hundred and twenty.

Register No. 107 Teste R Turnbull CC

Brunswick County Court 25th October 1820

The above certificate was compared with the person of the said JINCEY LANTY and found to be correct.

Teste R Turnbull CBC

=====

Brunswick County to wit
I do hereby certify that the bearer hereof PATTY a free woman of colour, about forty eight years old, five feet six Inches high, and of a dark complexion, has one scar on the fore Finger of the left hand, no scar on the face, head, hands & arms perceivable, and is one of the slaves emancipated by the last Will & Testament of CREED HASKINS SR. deceased, which is duly recorded in this Court. Given under my hand this 25th March 1821.

Register No. 108 Teste R Turnbull CC
Geo Hardeway JP
Brunswick County March Term 1821
The above certificate was compared with the person of the said PATTY & found correct.
Teste R Turnbull CC

=====

Brunswick County to wit
I do hereby certify that the bearer hereof ELIZA a free woman of colour, about twenty one years old, 5 feet 6½ Inches high and of a bright complexion, has no scar or marks on her head, face, hands or arms perceivable and is one of the Slaves emancipated by the last Will and Testament of CREED HASKINS SR. Given under my hand 25th March 1821

Register No. 109 Teste R Turnbull CC
Geo Hardaway JP
Brunswick County March 26th 1821
The above certificate was compared with the person of the said ELIZA and found to be correct.
Teste R Turnbull

=====

Brunswick County to wit
I do hereby certify that the bearer hereof NANCY a free woman of Colour, about 17 years old 5 feet high & of a bright complexion, has no scar or mark on the face, head, hands or arms, perceivable & is one of the Slaves emancipated by the last Will and Testament CREED HASKINS SR. decd.

Register No. 110 Teste R Turnbull CC
Geo Hardaway JP
Brunswick County 26th March 1821
The above certificate was examined & found to be correct.
Teste R Turnbull CC

=====

Brunswick County to wit

I do hereby certify that the bearer hereof LUD WALKER a free man of colour about twenty one years of age 5 F 10 I high and of a bright complexion, has a scar on the left arm just below the Elbow & another on the wrist of the right arm, & was born free in this County. Given under my hand the 25th March 1821.

Teste R Turnbull CC

Register No 111
Geo Hardaway JP

Brunswick County Ct. 26th March 1821

The above certificate was compared with the person of the said WALKER and found to be correct.

Teste R Turnbull CC

=====

Brunswick County to wit

I do hereby certify that the bearer hereof CHARLES WALKER a free man of colour, about twenty eight years of age, five feet five inches high, has three scars or marks perceivable, two of which are on his left Arm and the other on his breast, and of a light complexion, who it appears was emancipated by the Exor of the last Will and Testament of WM WALKER decd. Given under my hand this 25th of March one thousand eight hundred and twenty one.

Register No. 112 Teste R Turnbull CBC

Brunswick County Court 27th March 1821

The above certificate was compared with the person of the said CHARLES WALKER decd. (sic) and found correct.

Teste R Turnbull CBC

=====

Brunswick County to wit

I do hereby certify that the bearer hereof HERBERT MOSS a free man of colour, about twenty four or five years of Age, five feet six Inches hight, has a scar occasioned by a scald under the Arm and near the wrist of the left hand, a mould on the wrist of the left hand near the Joint of the thumb, who it appears was emancipated by HENRY MORRISS. Given under my hand this 25th day of March one thousand eight hundred and twenty one.

Register No. 113 Teste R Turnbull CC

Brunswick County Court 27th March 1821

The foregoing certificate was compared with the person of the said MOSS & found correct.

Teste R Turnbull CC

=====

Brunswick County to wit
I do hereby certify that the bearer hereof JOSEPH JONES a free man of colour about twenty two or three years of age five feet 8½ inches high and of a light complexion, who was free born as free born as appears by the evidence of WILLIAM YATES. Given under my hand his 25th March 1821.

Register No. 114 Teste R Turnbull
Brunswick County Court March 27th 1821
The above certificate was compared with the person of the said JONES and found correct. Teste R Turnbull CC

=====

Brunswick County to wit
I do hereby certify that the bearer hereof ARTHUR WALKER a free man of colour about twenty five years of age, 5 9½ high has a mark or scar on the nuckle of the forefinger of the right hand, no other mark or scar on the face, head, hands or arms perceivable, who was emancipated by the Exor of the last Will & Testament of WM WALKER dec'd. Given under my hand 25th March 1821

Register No. 115 Teste R Turnbull CBC
Brunswick County Court 25th March 1821
The above certificate was compared with the person of the said WALKER & found to be correct.
Teste R Turnbull CC

=====

State of Virginia Greensville County Court Clerks Office 13th day of December 1820
No. 78 JUDY GRAVES, a free negro woman emancipated by RICHARD GRAVES of Dinwiddie of a dark complexion, aged about forty five years, five feet two & 3/4 inches high (in shoes) by occupation a weaver her little finger on her right hand crooked from a sprain. Registered at her request at my Office the above day & date. In testimony where of I have herewith set my hand & Affixed the County seal.
Edmund Mason CGC

The above register examined & approved by me a justice of the peace for the County of Greensville this 13th day of December 1820.
Nat. Land JP

The foregoing certificate was registered in the Clerks Office of Brunswick the 28th day of May 1821.
Teste R Trunbull CBC

=====

Brunswick County to wit

I do hereby certify that the bearer hereof STEPHEN a black man of about thirty five years of age five feet four Inches high, a scar over the right eye five flesh moles on the breast & 7 moles on the back & shoulders, and a mould under the left year obtained his freedom in the Superior Court of Brunswick by a suit in said Court against the Exor of HERBERT HILL decd. Given under my hand this 25th June 1821

Registered No. 116 R Turnbull

Brunswick County June Court 1821

The above certificate was compared with the person of the said STEPHEN & found correct.

R Turnbull CC

=====

Brunswick County to wit

I do hereby certify that the bearer hereof ENOS EASTARD a free man a free man (sic) of colour, about thirty years of age five feet 10¼ Inches high has but one scar perceivable, which a burn on the left side of the neck, which said ENOS was emancipated by the last Will & Testament of OWEN MYRICK dec'd which is duly recorded in the Court of said County. Given under my hand this 23rd day of June 1821

Registered No. 117 R Turnbull CC

Brunswick County Court June 25th 1821

The above certificate was compared with the person of the said ENOS & found to be correct.

R Turnbull

=====

Brunswick County to wit

I do hereby certify that the bearer hereof BETSEY ROBERTS a free man (sic) of colour about 21 years of age 5 3½ Inches high has a scar on the left writ, which said BETSEY was born free as appears from the evidence of (no name). Given under my hand the 23rd June 1821.

Registered No. 118 R Turnbull

Brunswick County June Court 1821

The above certificate was compared with the person of the said BETSEY & found to be correct.

Teste R Turnbull

=====

Brunswick County to wit
I do hereby certify that the bearer hereof MARY JONES a free woman of colour about twenty six years old 5.6 Inches high, has a scar on the left hand, one on the left cheek and another on the forehead and was emancipated by the Will of OWEN MYRICK dec'd. which is duly recorded in the Clerks Office of said Court. Given under my hand this 23rd June 1821.

Register No. 119 Teste R Turnbull CC

Brunswick County June Court 1821

The above certificate was compared with the person of the said MARY & found to be correct.

Teste R Turnbull CC

=====

Brunswick County to wit
I do hereby certify that the bearer hereof AUSTIN a free man of colour about 43 years old 5.7 high has a scar on the right jaw, no other scar or mark on his head, face, hand or arms percei-vable, by occupation a sawyer, who was emancipated by EDWARD DROMGOOLE SR. by deed of emancipation duly recorded in the Court of said County. Given under my hand this 23rd June 1821

Registered No. 120 R Turnbull CC

Brunswick County June Court 1821

The above certificate was compared with the person of sd AUSTIN & found to be correct.

Teste R Turnbull CC

=====

Brunswick County to wit
I do hereby certify that the bearer hereof CLARISSA EASTARD a free woman of colour, about 34 years old 5 F 1½ I high, has no scar or mark perceivable on her head, face, hands or arms & was emancipated by the last Will & Testament of OWEN MYRICK dec'd. Given under my hand this the 23rd June 1821

Register No. 121 R Turnbull CC

Brunswick County June Court 1821

The above certificate was compared with the person of the said CLARISSA & found to be correct.

Teste R Turnbull CC

=====

Brunswick County to wit

I do hereby certify that the bearer hereof BEN, alias BEN LEWIS, a free man of a black complection about 26 years of age 6 F ½ I high, has no scar or mark on his head, hands, arms or face & was free born in this County as appears from the evidence of JAMES ELMORE. Given under my hand this 25th June 1821.

Register No. 122 R Turnbull

Brunswick County June Court

The above certificate was compared with the person of the said BEN & found to be correct.

Teste R Turnbull CC

=====

Brunswick County to wit

I do hereby certify that the bearer hereof SALLY alias SALLY HUNT a free woman of colour about 28 years of age, 5 5½ high, has no scar or mark perceivable & was emancipated by JOHN BREWER of this County by deed of emancipation duly recorded in the Court of said County. Given under my hand this 25th June 1821.

Register No. 123 R Turnbull

Brunswick County June Court 1821

The above certificate was compared with the person of the said SALLY and found to be correct.

Teste R Turnbull CC

=====

Brunswick County to wit

I do hereby certify that the bearer hereof BETTY alias (BETTY HUNT, a free woman of colour about 60 years of age 5 9 high no scar or mark perceivable on her head, face, hands or arms and was emancipated by JOHN BREWER of said County by Deed of emancipation duly recorded in the Court of said County. Given under my hand the 25th June 1821.

R Turnbull

Register No. 124

Brunswick County Court June 25th 1821

The above certificate was compared with the person of said BETTY & found correct.

Teste R Turnbull CC

=====

Brunswick County to wit

I do hereby certify that the bearer hereof MARY alias, MARY HUNT, a free woman of colour about 12 years old 5 8½ Inches high has a small scar under the right eye, no other perceivable, was emancipated by JOHN BREWER by deed of emancipation duly recorded in the Court of said County. Given under my hand this 25th June 1821.

Registered No. 125 R Turnbull CC

Brunswick County June Court 1821

The above certificate was compared with the person of the said MARY and found to be correct.

~~Registered No. 126~~ (sic) R. Turnbull

=====

Brunswick County to wit

I do hereby certify that the bearer hereof DAVID alias DAVID HUNT a free man of a yellowish complexion about 28 years old 5. 11½ Inches has a scar or mark perceivable on his left hand by occupation a carpenter & was emancipated by JOHN BREWER of this County by deed of emancipation duly recorded in the Court of said County. Given under my hand this 25 June 1821.

Registered No. 126 R Turnbull CC

Brunswick County June Court 1821

This Certificate was compared with the person of the said DAVID and found correct.

Teste R Turnbull CC

=====

Brunswick County to wit

I do hereby certify that the bearer hereof KITT alias, KITT HUNT, a free man of colour, about twenty five years of age 5.9 Inches high of a yellowish complexion, has a scar on all four fingers of his right hand just below the first Joint, who was emancipated by JOHN BREWER by Deed of emancipation duly recorded in the Court of said County. Given under my hand this 25 June 1821.

Register No. 127 R Turnbull CC

Brunswick County Court June 25th 1821

The above certificate was compared with the person of the said KITT & found to be correct.

Teste R Turnbull CC

=====

Brunswick County to wit
I do hereby certify that the bearer hereof BETSEY WALKER a free woman of colour about five feet 5½ high 17 years old black complexion a scar on the right side of the neck, was free born as appears from the evidence of WILLIAM PALMER. Given under my hand the 25th June 1821

Register No. 128 R Turnbull CC
Brunswick County June Court 1821
The above certificate was compared with the person of the said BETSEY & found to be correct.
R Turnbull

=====

Brunswick County to wit
I do hereby certify that the bearer hereof CLARISSA WALKER a free woman of colour of a black complexion 5 F ½ I high 24 years old & all the fingers & thumb of the right hand made stiff by a burn, and was born free as appears from the evidence of WM PALMER. Given under my hand this 25th June 1821.

Register No. 129 R Turnbull CC
Brunswick County June Court 1821
The above certificate was compared with the person of the said CLARISSA & found to be correct.
Teste R Turnbull CC

=====

Brunswick County S ct.
I do hereby certify that the bearer hereof BOB alias BOB WOODLIEF a free man of colour about thirty nine years of age 5 F 4½ I high, of a yellow complection, has a scar on the left year (a piece of his year from appearance seems to have been cut or bit off) & another scar on the back of the left hand, scarcely worthy of notice, who is one of the slaves emancipated by EDWARD DROMGOOLE SR by deed of emancipation duly recorded in the Court of said County. Given under my hand this 23rd day of July 1821.

Register No. 130 R Turnbull CC
Brunswick County July Court 1821
The above certificate was compared with the person of said BOB & found to be correct.
Teste R Turnbull CC

=====

Brunswick County S ct.

I do hereby certify that the bearer hereof DANIEL, a free man of colour, about 48 years old, of a yellow complection 5 F 7 or 8 I high, has a scar or mark below the left eye no mark on his hands or arms, & is one of the slaves emancipated by EDWARD DROMGOOLE SR by Deed of emancipation duly recorded in the Court of said County. Given under my hand this 23rd day of July 1821

Register No. 131 R Turnbull CC

Brunswick County July Court 1821

The above certificate was compared with the person of said DANIEL & found to be correct

Teste R Turnbull CC

=====

Brunswick County S ct.

I do hereby certify that the bearer hereof POLLY WALKER a free woman of colour about 18 years of age 5 F 5 I high, yellow complection a scar just below the elbow of the left arm, & another small one on the back part of the neck, was born free as appears by satisfactory evidence to the Court. Given under my hand this 23rd July 1821

Register No 132 R Turnbull CC

Brunswick County Court 23rd July 1821

The above certificate was compared with the person of the said POLLY & found to be correct

Teste R Turnbull CC

=====

Brunswick County S ct.

I do hereby certify that the bearer hereof ELIZA a free woman of colour, about 20 years of age 5 6½ I high yellow complection, h a small scar on the back of the right hand, was born free as appears from satisfactory evidence to the Jury. Given under my hand this 23rd day of July 1821.

Register No. 133 R Turnbull CC

Brunswick County July Court 1821

The above certificate was compared with the person of the said ELIZA and found to be correct.

Teste R Turnbull CC

=====

Brunswick County S ct.

I do hereby certify that the bearer hereof LEWIS a free man of colour about 5.4 high of a black complection, forty six years old, has a scar on the left year , & another between the wrist & nuckle of the thumb on the left hand was emancipated by Deed of emancipation duly recorded in the Court of said County. Given under my hand this 23rd July 1821

Register No. 134 R Turnbull CC

Brunswick County Court 23rd July 1821

The above certificate was compared with the person of the said LEWIS & found to be correct

Teste R Turnbull CC

=====

(Note: Starred Register Numbers are duplicates.)

Brunswick County to wit

I do hereby certify that the bearer hereof ADAM, alias ADAM ABRAM, about 49 years old 5 11½ Inches high has a small scar just below the thumb of the right hand was emancipated by EDWARD DROMGOOLE SR of this County by deed of emancipation duly recorded in the Court of this County. Given under my hand this 25th June 1821

Register No. 125* R Turnbull

Brunswick County June Court 1821

The above certificate was compared with the person of the said ADAM & found to be correct

=====

Brunswick County to wit

I do hereby certify the bearer hereof BOATSWAIN a free man of colour, about 54 years of age, 5 F 5½ I high has a small scar on the under lip, and on his his (sic) right a scar from a burn, was emancipated by EDWARD DROMGOOLE SR by deed of emancipation duly recorded in this Court. Given under my hand this 28th August 1821

Register No. 126* R Turnbull CC

Brunswick County Court August 29th 1821

The above certificate was compared with the person & found to be correct

Teste R Turnbull CC

=====

Brunswick County S ct.

I do hereby certify that the bearer hereof ELIJAH LEWIS a free man of colour about twenty one years of age 6 feet high has a scar on his left thumb, no other scar or mark perceivable on his head, hands, face or arms, and by occupation a ditcher, was born free in thi County as appears by the evidence of GEORGE STAINBACK. Given under my hand this 27th August 1821

Registered No. 127* R Turnbull CC

Brunswick County August Term 1821

The above certificate was compared with the person of the said ELIJAH LEWIS & found to be correct

Teste R Turnbull CC

=====

Brunswick County S ct.

I do hereby certify that the bearer hereof BEN JONES, a free man of colour about 20 years of age 5 10 high, has a small scar on the middle knuckle of the middle finger of the left hand, no other scar or mark perceivable on his head, hands, arms or face was born free in this County as appears by the evidence of THOMAS CHEELY. Given under my hand this 24th of September 1821

Register No. 128* R Turnbull CC
Willie Harrison JP

Brunswick County Ct. September Term 1821

The above certificate was compared by the Court & found to be correct

Teste R Turnbull CC

=====

Brunswick County S ct

I do hereby certify that the bearer hereof PHEBE a free woman of colour of a yellow complection, twenty one years of age, 5 1½ high, has a scar under the right eye, several others on the left arm, both above & below the elbow was emancipated by BENJAMIN JONES of this County, Given under my hand the 24th September 1821.

Registered No. 129* R Turnbull CC
Willie Harrison JP

Brunswick County Court September Term 1821

The above certificate was compared with the person of the said PHEBE & found to be correct

Teste R Turnbull CC

=====

Brunswick County S ct.

I do hereby certify that the bearer hereof DELILAH, a free woman of colour of a yellow complection, about 25 years age 5 F ½ I high, has no scar or mark on her head, hands, arms or face, is one of the slaves emancipated by BENJAMIN JONES of this County. Given under my hand this 24th September 1821

Registered No 130* R Turnbull CC
Willie Harrison JP

Brunswick County Court September Term 1821

The above certificate was compared with the person of the said DELILAH & found to be correct

Teste R Turnbull

=====

Brunswick County S ct.

I do hereby certify that the bearer hereof ROGER a free man of colour about 5 F 5 I high, 40 years of age has a scar on the thumb & wring finger of the left hand & another on the forefinger of the right hand was emancipated by OWEN MYRICK dec'd late of this County. Given under my hand this 22nd October 1821

Registered No. 131* R Turnbull CC

Brunswick County Court October 22nd 1821

The above certificate was compared with the person of the said ROGER & found to be correct

Teste R Turnbull CC

=====

Brunswick County S ct;

I do hereby certify that the bearer hereof FREEMAN WALKER a free man of colour about 22 years of age 5 F 8½ I high has a scar on the wrist of the right arm was born free as appears from the evidence of WILLIAM BALERIER (?). Given under my hand this 22nd day of October 1821

Registered No. 132* R Turnbull
John Tucker JP

Brunswick County Court October 22nd 1821

The above certificate was compared with the person of the said FREEMAN WALKER & found to be correct

Teste R Turnbull CC

=====

Brunswick County S ct
I do hereby certify that the bearer hereof MARIA WALKER a free woman of colour, yellow complexion, about 23 years old, five feet three & ½ Inches high has a scar just below and another above the elbow of the right arm, no other scar or mark perceivable on her head face hands or arms, was emancipated by WILLIAM WALKER late of this County appears by the evidence of WM SCARBOROUGH. Given under my hand this 25th day of January 1822.

Registered No. 133* R Turnbull cc

Brunswick County Court February 25th 1822
The above certificate was compared with the person of the said MARIA & found to be correct.

Teste R Turnbull CC

=====

Brunswick County S ct
I do hereby certify that the bearer hereof FLORA WALKER a free woman of colour, black complexion about 33 years old four feet 10½ Inches high, the thumb of the left hand and middle finger of the right hand stiff has no other moles mark or scar perceivable on her head face hands, arms or face, was emancipated by WM WALKER late of this County as appears by the evidence of WM SCARBOROUGH. Given under my hand this 28th January 1822

Register No 134* Teste R Turnbull cc

Brunswick County Court February 25th 1822
The above Certificate was compared with the person of the said FLORA & found to be correct.

Teste R Turnbull cc

=====

Brunswick County Sc
I do hereby certify that the bearer hereof LUKE MATTHEWS a free man of colour, yellow complexion about 5.9 Inches high 38 or 39 years old has a scar near midway between his eyes, another on the thumb of the left hand near & adjoining the nail, one about the Joint of the thumb with the hand of the same arm & another about the Joint, (inside), no other noted scar or mark perceivable. Given under my hand this 28th day of January 1822.

Registered No. 135 R Turnbull C

Brunswick County Court February 25th 1822
The above certificate was compared with the person of the said LUKE & found to be correct.

Teste R Turnbull CC

=====

Brunswick County S ct

I do hereby certify that the bearer hereof WILLIAM JONES a free man of colour about 22 years of age 5.9 high has a small scar on the right side of the left eye, yellow complexion was emancipated by BENJA. JONES dec'd late of this County as appears by the evidence of JOS. CHEELY. Given under my hand the 28th day of January 1822

Registered No. 136 R Turnbull CC

Brunswick County Court February 25 1822

The above certificate was compared with the person of the said WM & found to be correct

Teste R Turnbull CC

=====

Brunswick County S ct

I do hereby certify that the bearer hereof HANNAH JONES a free woman of colour, of a yellow complexion, about 33 years of age 5 5¼ Inches high, has a scar on the left side of the little finger of the left hand on the Joint that joins the hand no other scar or marks on her head face hands or arms perceivable was emancipated by BENJAMIN JONES late of this County as appears by the evidence of JOSEPH CHEELY. Given under my hands this 28th day of January 1822.

Registered No. 137 R Turnbull CC

Brunswick County Court February 25th 1822

The above certificate was compared with the person of the said HANNAH & found to be correct.

Teste R Turnbull CC

=====

Brunswick County S c

I do hereby certify that the bearer hereof SUCKEY WALKER a free woman of colour, dark complexion about five feet 4 or 5 Inches high, has several scars on the right arm near & about the elbow, about fifty one years of age, who is one of the slaves emancipated by the Will of WILLIAM WALKER late of this County as appears by the evidence of WM SCARBOROUGH. Given under my hand this 25th day of February 1822

Registered No. 138 R Turnbull CC

Brunswick County Court February 25th 1822

The above certificate was compared with the person of the said SUCKEY & found to be correct.

Teste R Turnbull CC

=====

Brunswick County to wit

This is to certify that the bearer hereof NED a free man of colour, about 21 years of age, 5.6½ inches high, has a scar under the left side of the Jaw, another under the right ear and two others on the neck, who was born free as appears from the evidence of JOHN WYCHE. Given under my hand this 23rd day of April 1822

Registered No. 139 R Turnbull CC
John B Rice JP

Brunswick County Court April 23rd 1822

The above certificate was compared with the person of the said NED and found to be correct

Teste R Turnbull CC

=====

Brunswick County to wit

This is to certify that the bearer hereof BETSEY MATTHEWS a free woman of colour about thirty years old 5.5 high and yellow complexion has a scar on the right arm between the wrist & elbow, and another near or on the right arm, and was born free in this County as appears from the evidence of RALEIGH H. ABERNATHY. Given under my hand this 24th June 1822

Registered No 140 R Turnbull CC
John Wyche JP

Brunswick county Court June 24th 1822

The above certificate was compared with the person of said BETSEY & found correct.

Teste R Turnbull CC

=====

Brunswick county to wit

I do hereby certify that the bearer hereof DAVID WALKER a free man of colour about 6 feet high black complexion, about 27 years of age, has a scar under the left jaw, another small one in the forehead was emancipated by PETER ROBERTSON Exor PETER JONES dec'd by deed of emancipation duly recorded in the County Court of Brunswick aforesaid. Given under my hand this 25th day of March 1822.

Register No. 141 R Turnbull CC
J. Rice JP

Brunswick County July Court 1822

The above certtificate was compared with the person of said DAVID WALKER and found to be correct.

Teste R Turnbull

=====

Brunswick County to wit
This is to certify that the bearer hereof AGGY WALKER a free woman of colour, about 5 F 4½ I high, thirty five years of age, has no scar or mark perceivable, was emancipated by WILLIAM WALKER dec'd by deed of emancipation duly recorded in the Clerks Office of said Court. Given under my hand this 23rd day of September 1822.

Registered No 142 R Turnbull
John Wyche JP

Brunswick County Court September 23rd 1822
The above certificate was compared with the person of said AGGY WALKER and found to be correct.

Teste R Turnbull

=====

Brunswick County to wit
I do hereby certify that the bearer hereof THOMAS LAWRENCE a mulatto man about thirty one years of age five feet ten Inches high of a bright complexion, has no scar or mark on his face head or hands or arms was born free as appears from the Evidence of _____ . Given under my hand this 23rd day of September 1822.

R Turnbull CC

Brunswick County September Court 1822
The above certificate compared & found to be correct.
John Wyche JP Registered No. 143.

=====

Brunswick County to wit
I do certify that the bearer hereof ELISHA WALKER a free man of colour, about 23 years of age, 5 feet 6½ Inches high and of a yellow complexion has a scar on the right side of the neck and no other on his head, face, hands or arms perceivable, and is one of the slaves emancipated by WILLIAM WALKER dec'd. as appears by the evidence of WILLIAM SCARBOROUGH. Given under my hand this 27th day of November 1822.

Registered No. 144 R Turnbull CC
James Wyche JP

Brunswick County Court November 27 1822
The above certificate was compared with the person of said ELISHA WALKER and found to be correct.

Teste R Turnbull CC

=====

Brunswick County to wit

I do hereby certify that the bearer hereof PETER a free man of colour, about 57 years of age, 5 F 9 I high and of a black complection has no scar or mark perceivable on head face hands or arms, and is the same negro PETER directed to be emancipated by the last Will and Testament of RICHD. CLARK dec'd at the death of his wife as appears by the evidence of NATHANIEL E. MALOY. Given under my hand this 26th day of November 1822.

Registered No. 145 R Turnbull CC

James Wyche JP

Brunswick County Court November 1822

The above certificate was compared with the person of said PETER & found to be correct.

Teste R Turnbull CC

=====

Brunswick County to wit

This is to certify that the bearer hereof DANIEL LEWIS a free man of colour about 61 years of age five feet 10½ Inches high has no particular scar on his face, head, hands or arms of thin visage, and by occupation a planter is one of the slave emancipated by the Will & Testament of OWEN MYRICK of record in this County. Given under my hand this 24th day of March 1823.

Registered No. 146 R Turnbull C

Brunswick County March Ct 1823

The above certificate compared with the person of said DANIEL & found to be correct.

Teste R Turnbull

=====

Brunswick County to wit

I do hereby certify that the bearer hereof ENOS a black man of a yellow complexion about forty two years of age 5 feet 4 or 5 Inches high has a scar on the back of the left hand occasioned by a cut has no scar perceivable on the face is one of the slaves emancipated by BENJAMIN JONES dec'd as appears by a certificate of his Executor. Given under my hand this 24th day of March 1823.

Registered No. 147 R Turnbull CC

Brunswick County March Court 1823

The above certificate was compared with the person of said ENOS & found to be correct.

J. Rice JP Teste R Turnbull CC

=====

Brunswick County to wit
I do hereby certify that the bearer hereof MARY JONES a free woman of colour about 28 years old 5 feet 6 Inches high has a scar on the left hand, one on the left cheek and another on the forehead, and emancipated by the will of OWEN MYRICK dec'd which is duly recorded in the Clerks Office of said County. Given under my hand this 24th day of March 1823.

Register No 148 R Turnbull CC
J. Rice JP
Brunswick County March Court 1823
The foregoing certificate was compared with the person of MARY JONES and found to be correct.
Teste R Turnbull CC

=====

Brunswick County to wit
I do certify that the bearer hereof NED JONES a free man of colour about fifty years of age, 5 feet 8 Inches high, dark complexion, has no mark or scar perceivable & is one of the slaves emancipated by BENJAMIN JONES dec'd as appears by the Evidence of ROBERT TURNBULL. Given under my hand this the 26th day of November 1822.

Register No. 149 R Turnbull CC
J H Chapman JP
Brunswick County November Court 1822

The above certificate was compared with the person of said NED JONES & found to be correct.
Teste R Turnbull CC

=====

Brunswick County to wit
I do hereby certify that the bearer hereof DICY a free woman of Colour, about thirty years of age five feet eight Inches high has a small scar in the nose between the eyes another on the forehead and one other on the left arm just above the wrist is one of the slaves emancipated by the will of OWEN MYRICK dec'd duly proved and recorded in this Court. Given under my hand the 25th of March 1823.

Registered No. 150
Brunswick County Court March 25th 1823
The above certificate of the person DICY was compared and found to be Correct.
Teste R Turnbull CC

=====

Brunswick County to wit

I do hereby certify that the bearer hereof JUDETH a woman of a light complexion about 25 years of age 5 feet high has a lengthy scar on the left arm occasioned by a cut was emancipated by BENJAMIN JONES dec'd by deed of Record in the Office. Given under my hand thi 24th day of March 1823.

Register No. 151 R Turnbull CC
J. Rice JP

Brunswick County March Court 1823
The above certificate was compared with the person of the said JUDETH and found to be correct.

Teste R Turnbull CC

=====

Brunswick County to wit

I do certify that the bearer hereof a black man named NED MOSS of a dark complexion about thirty three years of age five feet nine inches high has a scar on the inside of the righ arm of just below the Elbow and other on the back of the left hand was born free as appears by the evidence of TILMAN AVERY in Court. Given under my hand this 26th May 1823.

Register No. 152 R Turnbull CC

Brunswick County Court May Term 1823
The above compared and found correct.

=====

Brunswick County to wit

I do certify that the bearer hereof HENRY CAIN of a black complexion between thirty & thirty five years of age about five feet six ½ Inches high has a scar just above the right Eye was free born as appears from the evidence of RICHARD FLETCHER and by Occupation a planter. Given under my hand this 23rd day of June 1823.

Register No. 153 R Turnbull CC
C Cordle JP

Brunswick County Court June 23rd 1823
The above compared & found to be correct.

=====

Brunswick County S ct
I do hereby Certify that the bearer hereof BENJAMIN JONES a free man of Colour Yellow Complexion about twenty one Years of age five feet nine Inches high has a scar under the right Jaw no other scar or mark on his head hands, arms or face perceivable was Emancipated by BENJA JONES dec'd late of this County as appears by the Evidence of AUGUSTIN C JONES. Given under my hand this 23rd day of June 1823.

Register No. 154 R Turnbull CC

Brunswick County Court June 23rd 1823
The above Certificate was Compared with the person & found to be Correct.

R Turnbull

=====

Brunswick County to wit
I do hereby Certify that the Bearer hereof PHILIS CAIN of a black Complexion about fifty two Years of age five feet four Inches high Emancipated by OWEN MYRICK by the Evidence of RICHARD FLETCHER. Given under my hand this 23rd day of June 1823.

Register No. 155 R Turnbull CC
Gray F. Dunn JP

Brunswick County Court June 23rd 1823
The above Certificate Compared & found to be Correct.

R Turnbull

=====

Brunswick County to wit
This is to Certify that the bearer hereof POLLY OWEN a free woman about forty seven Years old five feet five & a half Inches high has no scar or marks worth mentioning except some on the forehead occasioned by the small pox & was born free as appears from the Evidence of DAVID B STITH. Given under my hand this 23rd day of June 1823.

Register No. 156 R Turnbull CC

Gray F Dunn JP

Brunswick County Court June 23rd 1823
The above Certificate Compared & found to be Correct.

R Turnbull CC

=====

Brunswick County to wit

This is to Certify that the bearer hereof JAROD EASTER a free man about thirty nine Years of age five feet nine Inches high has but one small scar which is just above the corner of the mouth no other perceivable and is one of the one (sic) slaves Emancipated by OWEN MYRICK dec'd as appears by the Evidence of RICHARD FLETCHER. Given under my hand this 23rd June 1823.

Register No. 157
Gray F Dunn J. P.

Brunswick County Court June 23rd 1823
The above Certified Compared & found to be Correct.

R Turnbull CC

=====

Brunswick County to wit;

This is to Certify that the bearer hereof MATT GRAIN a free man about forty five Years of age five feet seven Inches high has a Cut on the left Ear no other scar or mark perceivable is one of the slaves emancipated by OWEN MYRICK dec'd late of this County as appears by the Evidence or RICHARD FLETCHER and by Occupation a Ditcher Given under my hand this 23rd June 1823.

Registered No. 158
Gray F Dunn JP

Brunswick County Court June 23rd 1823
The above Certificate Compared & found to be Correct.

R Turnbull CC

=====

Brunswick County to wit

This is to Certify that the bearer hereof BERRY ROBERTS a free man about twenty three years of age five feet six Inches high no scar or mark perceivable was free born as appears from the Evidence of RICHARD FLETCHER. Given under my hand this 23rd day of June 1823

Registered No. 159 R Turnbull CC
Gray F Dunn JP

Brunswick County Court June 23rd 1823
The above Certificate Compared & found to be Correct.

R Turnbull CC

=====

Brunswick County to wit

This is to Certify that the bearer hereof ANDREW CAIN a free man about forty Years of age five feet three Inches high has no scar or mark perceivable and is one of the slaves Emancipated by OWEN MYRICK dec'd as appears by the Evidence of RICHARD FLETCHER. Given under my hand this 23rd day of June 1823.

Register No 160 R Turnbull CC
Gray F Dunn JP

Brunswick County Court June 23rd 1823

The above Certificate Compared with the person & found Correct.

R Turnbull CC

=====

Brunswick County to wit

This is to Certify that the bearer hereof LEWIS ROBERTS a free man about fifty three Years of age five feet nine Inches high has a scar on the right arm between the wrist & the Elbow occasioned by a burn by Occupation a Cooper & is one of the slaves Emancipated by OWEN MYRICK dec'd as appears from the Evidence of RICHARD FLETCHER. Given under my hand this 23rd day of June 1823.

Register No. 161 R Turnbull CC
Gray F Dunn JP

Brunswick County Court June 23rd 1823

The above Certificate was Compared with the person & found to be correct.

R Turnbull CC

=====

Brunswick County to wit

This is to Certify that the bearer hereof SOPHIA ROBERTS about Eighteen Years of age five feet two Inches high has no scar or mark perceivable and was born free as appears by the Evidence of RICHARD FLETCHER. Given under my hand this 23rd June 1823.

Register No. 162 R Turnbull CC
Gray F Dunn JP

Brunswick County Court June 23rd 1823

The above Certificate was Compared & found to be Correct.

R Turnbull CC

=====

Brunswick County to wit
This is to Certify that the bearer hereof HANNAH ROBERTS about thirty years of age five feet five Inches high has a scar on the left arm occasioned by a burn and was Emancipated by OWEN MYRICK dec'd as appears by the Evidence of RICHARD FLETCHER. Given under my hand this 23rd June 1823.

Register No. 162* R Turnbull
Gray F Dunn JP
Brunswick County Court June 23rd
The above Certificate & found to be correct. (Sic)
R Turnbull

=====

Brunswick County to wit
I do hereby Certify that the bearer hereof STEPHEN MALONE a free man of Yellow complexion about twenty four Years old five feet 6¼ Inches high, the fingers of the left hand are stiff caused (as he says) by the rheumatism has two small scars on the forehead & several others on the face was born free as appears by the Evidence of JOHN P. MALONE and by Occupation a planter. Given under my hand this 23rd day of June 1823.

Registered No. 164 R Turnbull CC
Gray F Dunn JP
Brunswick County Court June 23rd 1823
The above Certificate Compare & found Correct.
R Turnbull

=====

Brunswick County to wit
This is to Certify that the bearer hereof JIM EASTER of a black Complexion about nineteen Years old six feet high has a scar on the back & another in the palm of the left hand & one other scar on the right wrist was born free as appears from the Evidence of RICHARD FLETCHER and by occupation a Ditcher. Given under my hand this 23rd day of June 1823.

Register No. 165 R Turnbull CC
Gray F Dunn JP
Brunswick County Court June 23rd 1823
The above Certificate Compared & found Correct.
R Turnbull CC

=====

Brunswick County to wit
I do hereby Certify that the bearer hereof JAMES CAIN of a black complexion about twenty eight Years of age five feet seven Inches high the fore finger on the right having been cut off was Emancipated by OWEN MYRICK Occupation a Sawyer as appears from Evidence of RICHARD FLETCHER. Given under my hand this 23rd June 1823.

Register No. 166 R Turnbull CC
Gray F Dunn JP

Brunswick County Court June 23rd 1823
This Certificate was Compared & found to be Correct.
R Turnbull

=====

Brunswick County to wit
This is to Certify that the bearer hereof BOB JAMES a free man of colour about fifty five Years old five feet seven Inches high has but one scar perceivable which is one the wright wrist & was emancipated by OWEN MYRICK dec'd late of this County as appears by Evidence of R FLETCHER. Given under my hand this 23rd day of June 1823.

Registered No. 167 R Turnbull CC
Gray F Dunn JP
Brunswick County Court June 23rd 1823
The Certificate Compared & found Correct.
R Turnbull CC

=====

Brunswick County to wit
I do hereby Certify that the bearer hereof NED JAMES of a black Complexion, about fifty five Years old five feet 8½ Inches high has no scar or mark worthy of notice except the little toe of the left foot is off and a small scar on the left hand by Occupation a planter is one of the slaves Emancipated by OWEN MYRICK late of this County as appears from Evidence of RICHARD FLETCHER. Given under my hand this 23rd day of June 1823.

Register No. 168 R Turnbull CC
Gray F Dunn JP
Brunswick County Court June 23rd 1823
The above Certificate was Compared & found Correct.
R Turnbull CC

=====

Brunswick County to wit
I do Certify that the bearer hereof ALLEN CAIN of a black Complexion about twenty one Years of age five feet ten ¼ Inches high has a scar on the right arm just above the wrist & also one other sca on the left arm just above the wrist and was free born as appears from the Evidence of RICHARD FLETCHER. Given under my hand this 23rd June 1823.

Register No. 169 R Turnbull CC
Gray F Dunn JP
Brunswick County June 23rd 1823
The above Certificate was Compared & found to be Correct.
R Turnbull CC

=====

Brunswick County to wit
I do Certify that the bearer hereof PETER CAIN of a black Complexion about twenty three or twenty four Years old five six & ½ Inches high has a scar on the back of the left hand & several other small scars on both hands & free born as appears from the Evidence of RICHARD FLETCHER. Given under my hand this 23rd day of June 1823.

Registered No. 170 R Turnbull CC
Gray F Dunn JP
Brunswick County Court June 23rd 1823
The above Certificate Compared & found Correct.
R Turnbull CC

=====

Brunswick County to wit
I do Certify that the bearer hereof JACOB WALKER a black man about twenty six Years of age five feet four Inches high, was born free as appears from the Evidence of CHARLES TUCKER by Occupation a planter. Given under my hand this 23rd day of June 1823.

Register No. 171 R Turnbull CC
John Wyche JP
Brunswick County Court June 23rd 1823
The above Certificate was Compared & found Correct.
R Turnbull CC

=====

Brunswick County to wit

This is to Certify that the bearer hereof HERBERT MOSS five feet six inches high (in shoes) about twenty seven Years of age light Complexion, has a scar occasioned by a scald under the arm near the wrist of the left hand and a mould on his left wrist near the joint of the thumb and as appears from the evidence of WM GEE is one of the Children who was emancipated by HARRY MOSS by Deed of emancipation duly recorded in the Court of Sussex County as appears by an attested Copy thereof. Given under my hand this 28th day of July 1823.

Register No. 172 R Turnbull
JAS. Rice JP

Brunswick County Court July 28th 1823
This Certificate was Compared with the person the said HERBERT MOSS & found to be Correct.

Teste R Turnbull CC

=====

Brunswick County to wit

This is to Certify that the bearer hereof FED commonly called WAGGONER FED, a black man about 48 years old 5 feet 5 inches high has a scar Just below the pit of the stomach occasioned by a stab has no scar or mark perceivable on his face head or arms and was emancipated by WILLIAM MEREDITH by deed of emancipation duly recorded in the Clerks Office of this County Court of Brunswick aforesaid. Given under my hand this 21st day of July 1823.

Register No. 173 R Turnbull CC

Brunswick County Court July 28th 1823
The above certificate compared & found to be correct.

Teste R Turnbull CC

=====

Brunswick County to wit

I do Certify that the bearer hereof JACK ROBERTS a free man of light Complexion about forty two Years of age five feet ten Inches has no scar perceivable was emancipated by OWEN MYRICK as appears from the evidence of RICHARD FLETCHER and by Occupation a Sawyer. Given under my hand this 25th day of August 1823.

Register No. 174

Brunswick County Court August 25th 1823
The above Certificate Compared with the person & found to be Correct.

R Turnbull Cl C

=====

Brunswick County to wit
I do hereby Certify that the bearer hereof GEORGE EASTER a free man of black Complexion five feet eight Inches high about twenty Years of age has no scar perceivable was born free as appears from the evidence of RICHARD FLETCHER and by occupation a Ditcher. Given under my hand this 25th day of August 1823.

Register No. 175 R Turnbull CC
Jas. Wyche JP
Brunswick County August Court 1823
The above Certificate Compared & found to be Correct.
R Turnbull CC

=====

Brunswick County to wit
I hereby Certify that the bearer hereof VIOLET GRAIN a free woman of Yellow Complexion about five feet three Inches high forty Years old has a small scar on the forehead occasioned by a cut was emancipated by OWEN MYRICK as appears from the evidence of RICHARD FLETCHER. Given under my hand this 25th day of Agust 1823.

Register No. 176 R Turnbull CC
Js. Rice JP
Brunswick County Court August Court 1823
The above Certificate Compared & found Correct.
R Turnbull CC

=====

Brunswick County to wit
This is to Certify that the bearer hereof ARTHUR a free man of black Complexion five feet nine Inches high has a scar on the left side of the face was emancipated by JOHN MASON of Greensville County as appears by an attested copy of the deed of emancipation. Given under my hand this 25th day of August 1823.

Register No. 177 R Turnbull Cl C
James Wyche JP
Brunswick County Court August 25th 1823
The above Certificate Compared & found Correct.
R Turnbull CC

=====

Brunswick County to wit

This is to Certify that the bearer hereof NANCY MALONE a free woman of Colour about 27 years of age five feet two & ¼ Inches high has a scar on the left side of the neck just under the jaw was born free as appears from the evidence of JOHN P MALONE. Given under my hand this 25th day of August 1823.

Register No. 178 R Turnbull CC
James Wyche JP

Brunswick County August Court 1823
The above Certificate Compared & found Correct.

R Turnbull CC

=====

Brunswick County to wit

This is to Certify that the bearer hereof ALLEN ATKINS a free man of Colour about twenty four Years of age five feet ten Inches high spare made has a very small scar on the forefinger of the left hand and another on the right hand near the thumb & forefinger both of which appear to have been caused by the cut of knife also a scar on the upper part of the neck a little space behind the right ear ap-apparently occasioned by a burn, which said ALLEN ATKINS was born free from the evidence of JOHN HARRISON. Given under my hand this 25th day of August 1823.

Register No. 179 R Turnbull
James Wyche JP

Brunswick County August Court 1823
The above Certificate Compared & found Correct.

R Turnbull Cl C

=====

Brunswick County to wit

This is to Certify that the bearer hereof POLLY alias POLLY MERRITT a free woman of a black Complexion was born free & served an apprenticeship with Mr. JOHN REEVES as appears from a Certificate from the Clerk of the County Court of Greensville five feet two Inches high & has on her upper lip a small scratch a small scar on her breast & a large one on her left elbow. Given under my hand this 25th day of August 1823.

Register No. 180 R Turnbull CC
Jas Wyche JP

Brunswick County August Court 1823
The above Certificate Compared and found Correct.

R Turnbull CC

=====

Brunswick County to wit

I hereby Certify that the bearer hereof ANN EASTER a free woman of a black Complexion five feet eight & a half Inches high about sixteen Years of age has no scar or mark perceivable was born free as appears from the evidence of RICHARD FLETCHER. Given under my hand this 25th day of August 1823.

Register No. 181 R Turnbull Cl C
James Wyche JP

Brunswick County August Court 1823
The above Certificate Compared & found to be Correct.
R Turnbull Cl C

=====

Brunswick County to wit

I do hereby Certify that the bearer hereof VILET GRAIN a free woman of dark Complexion five feet two Inches high about 19 Years old has no scar or mark perceivable was born free as appears from the evidence of RICHARD FLETCHER. Given under my hand this 25th day of August 1823.

Register No. 182 R Turnbull CC
Js.Rice JP

Brunswick County August Court 1823
The above Certificate & found to be Correct.
R Turnbull CC

=====

Brunswick County

I do hereby Certify that the bearer hereof SALLY GRAIN a free woman of black Complexion about five feet four Inches high forty Years of age has a scar on the left arm occasioned by a burn and on the left leg occasioned by the bite of a dog & no other scar or mark perceivable was emancipated by OWEN MYRICK as appears from the evidence of RICHARD FLETCHER. Given under my hand this 25th day of August 1823.

Register No. 183 R Turnbull CC
James Wyche JP

Brunswick County August Court 1823
The above Certificate Compared & found Correct.
R Turnbull

=====

Brunswick County to wit
This is to Certify that the bearer hereof DEMPSEY EASTER a free Man of a black Complexion about thirty two Years of age six feet one Inch high has a scar a little under the right temple one on the breast and several others near & about the left wrist and is one of the Slaves emancipated by OWEN MYRICK dec'd as appears by the evidence of RICHARD FLETCHER and by Occupation a Sawyer. Given under my hand this 28th day of July 1823.

Register No 184 R Turnbull CC
James Wyche JP
Brunswick County August Court 1823
The above Certificate Compared & found Correct.
R Turnbull CC

=====

Brunswick County to wit
I do hereby Certify that the bearer hereof BILLY GRAIN a free man of Yellow Complexion five feet seven & a half Inches high about twenty four years of age has a scar on the forehead occasioned by a Cut & one on the bottom of the left foot from a cut also and no other scar perceivable was born free as appears from the evidence of RICHARD FLETCHER and by Occupation a Sawyer. Given under my hand this 25th day of August 1823.

Register No. 185 R Turnbull
James Wyche JP
Brunswick County August Court 1823
The above Certificate Compared & found Correct.
R Turnbull CC

=====

Brunswick County to wit
I hereby Certify that the bearer hereof JAMES MERRITT a free man of black Complexion five feet 11 Inches high about thirty five Years of age has a small scar on the left arm occasioned by the Cut of a Scythe and two fingers Cut on the same hand by a Scythe (also) was emancipated by HENRY MERRITT as appears from the evidence of _______ and by occupation a Sawyer. Given under my hand this 25th day of August 1823.

Register No. 186 R Turnbull
James Wyche JP
Brunswick County August Court 1823
The above Certificate Compared & found to be Correct.
R Turnbull CC

=====

Brunswick County to wit

I do hereby Certify that the bearer hereof NANCY AVENT a free woman of Yellow Complexion five feet four Inches high about nineteen Years Old has a small scar in the forehead Occasioned by a fall and one on the arm occasioned by a Cut and no other scar or mark perceivable was born free as appears from the evidence of GRAY FINCH. Given under my hand this 25th day of August 1823.

Register No. 187 R Turnbull CC
James Wyche JP

Brunswick County August Court 1823
The above Certificate Compared & found Correct.

R Turnbull CC

=====

Brunswick County S ct.

This is to Certify that the bearer hereof BENJA. ROBERTS a free man of Colour about Twenty one Years of age five feet five & an half Inches has no scar or mark on his head, face hands or arms, except a very small one on the forehead a little to the right side, also on the right arm and wrist and also on the left elbow, was born free as appears from the evidence of JOHN PHIPPS, and by Occupation a carpenter. Given under my hand this 28th day of July 1823.

Registered No. 188 R Turnbull
Jas Wyche JP

Brunswick County Court August 25 1823
The above Certificate Compared and found Correct.

R Turnbull CC

=====

Brunswick County to wit

I do Certify that the bearer hereof ROGER CAIN a free man of Dark Complexion about five feet five Inches high forty three Years of Age has two small scars on the right arm occasioned by a scratch and also one on the left leg occasioned by a burn and no other scar perceivable was emancipated by OWEN MYRICK as appears from the evidence of RICHARD FLETCHER and by Occupation a farmer. Given under my hand this 25th day of August 1823.

Register No. 189 R Turnbull CC
James Wyche JP

Brunswick County August 1823
The above Certificate Compared & found Correct.

R Turnbull CC

=====

Brunswick County to wit

This is to certify that the bearer hereof DOSTIN POMPY a free man of Yellow complexion, about twenty one Years of Age Six feet high has a scar on the right arm and one other on the middle finger of the right hand was born free as appears from the evidence of PHILL CLAIBORNE and by Occupation a Carpenter. Given under my hand this 28th day of July 1823.

Register No. 190 R Turnbull CC
James Wyche JP

Brunswick County August Court 1823
The above Certificate Compared & found Correct.
R Turnbull Cl C

=====

Brunswick County to wit

I do hereby Certify that the bearer hereof BILLY STEWART a free man of black complexion six feet & an half Inch high about thirty Years of age has a scar on the left arm occasioned by a Cut of knife & no other scar perceivable was born free as appears from the evidence of PHIL CLAIBORNE and by Occupation a carpenter. Given under my hand this 28th day of August 1823.

Register No. 191 R Turnbull CC
James Wyche JP

Brunswick County August Court 1823
The above Certificate Compared & found to be Correct.
R Turnbull Cl C

=====

Brunswick County to wit

I do hereby Certify that the bearer hereof CLAIBORNE POMPY a free man of black Complexion five feet 8 Inches high about thirty five Years old has no scar perceivable was born free as appears from the evidence of PHIL CLAIBORNE and by Occupation a farmer. Given under my hand this 25th day of August 1823.

Register No. 192 R Turnbull Cl C
James Wyche JP

Brunswick County August Court 1823
The above Certificate Compared & found to be Correct.
R Turnbull Cl C

=====

Brunswick County to wit

This is to Certify that the bearer hereof EDMUND HARRISON a free man of Yellow Complexion about twenty two Years old five feet six & an half Inches high has a small scar on the right side of the nose & was born free as appears from the evidence of PHIL CLAIBORNE. Given under my hand this 28th day of July 1823.

R Turnbull CC

Register No. 193
James Wyche

Brunswick County August Court 1823
The above Certificate Compared & found Correct.

R Turnbull CC

=====

Brunswick County S ct

I do Certify that the bearer hereof BILLY a free man of colour of a black complection 32 years old, about 5.3 or 4 Inches high has 2 small scars on the inside of the right arm and two on the back of the right hand and wrist was born free in this County is the son of MARIA a free woman emancipated by HENRY MERRITT of this County. Given under my hand this the 20th Sept 1823.

Registered No. 194 R Turnbull CC

Brunswick County Court September 22nd 1823
The above certificate compared & found to be correct.
James Wyche JP Teste R Turnbull

=====

Brunswick County to wit

I do certify that the bearer hereof ISAAC MOSS a free man of colour, dark complexion 5.7½ Inches high about 25 years old has a long scar on the under part of his left wrist and two small ones on the ball of the thumb of the left hand was born free in this County. Given under my hand this the 20th day of September 1823.

Register No. 195 R Turnbull

Brunswick County Court September 22nd 1823
The above certificate was compared with the person of said ISAAC MOSS & found to be correct.
James Wyche JP Teste R Turnbull

=====

Virginia Brunswick County to wit

I do certify that the bearer hereof DILCEY a free woman of colour about 55 years old 5 F 2 or 3 I high has several scars on the right arm and one on the left is one of the slaves emancipated by HENRY MOSS late of the County of Sussex as appears by the evidence of WILLIAM GEE. Given under my hand this 20th day of September 1823.

Registered No. 196 R Turnbull CBC

Brunswick County Court September 22nd 1823

The above certificate was compared with the person of said DILCY and found to be correct.

James Wyche JP R Turnbull CC

=====

Brunswick County to wit

The bearer hereof DAVID MERRITT a free man of colour about 26 years of age 5 F 9 I high has a scar on the right side of the Jaw was born free and is the son of MARIA one of the slaves emancipated by HENRY MERRITT of this county. Given under my hand this 22nd September 1823

Register No. 197 R Turnbull CC

Brunswick County Court September 22nd 1823

The above certificate was compared with the person of said DAVID & found to be correct.

James Wyche JP Teste R Turnbull CC

=====

Brunswick County to wit

I do certify that the bearer hereof PATSEY a free woman of colour, about 5 feet high & 24 years old has a scar on the forefinger of the left hand was born free in this County and is a daughter of FED, otherwise called WAGGONER FED, who was emancipated by WILLIAM MEREDITH. Given under my hand this 20 September 1823.

Register No. 198 R Turnbull CC

Brunswick County Court September 22 1823

The above certificate was compared with the person of said PATSEY and found to be correct.

James Wyche J.P. Teste R Turnbull CC

=====

Brunswick County to wit
I do certify that the bearer hereof POLLY a free woman of colour 5 F 0½ I high about 25 years old has a small scar on the back of the left hand was born free in this County and is a daughter of FED, otherwise called WAGGONER FED, who was Emancipated by WILLIAM MEREDITH. Given under my hand this 20th day of September 1823.

Register No. 199 R Turnbull CC

Brunswick County Court September 22 1823
The above certificate was compared with the person of said POLLY and found to be correct.

Teste R Turnbull CC

=====

Brunswick County to wit
I do certify that the bearer hereof AGGY a free woman of colour, of a yellow complection, 4 F 10½ I high about 48 years old has no scar or mark on her face hands or arms perceivable was borne free in the County of Dinwiddie but has (sic) in this County for several years last past and is the reputed wife FED, (otherwise called WAGGONER FED), a free black man emancipated by WILLIAM MEREDITH. Given under my hand this 20th September 1823.

Register No. 200 R Turnbull CC

BrunsK. County Sept Ct. 1823
The above Certif. compared & found correct.
James Wyche JP R Turnbull CC

=====

Brunswick County to wit
I do hereby certify that the bearer hereof SALLY a free woman of colour 4 F: 11 I high about 23 years old has no scar on her face head hands nor arms, perceivable was born free in this County and is a daughter of FED (otherwise called WAGGONER FED) who was emancipated by WILLIAM MEREDITH. Given under my hand this 20th September 1823.

Register No. 201 R Turnbull CC

Brunswick County Court September 22nd 1823
The above certificate was compared with the person of said SALLY and found to be correct.
James Wyche JP Teste R Turnbull CC

=====

Brunswick County to wit

I do certify that HARTWELL a free man of colour yellow complexion, about six feet high, and nineteen years of age, has a scar on the chin & another on the little finger of the left hand, and is a descendant of one of the slaves emancipated by EDWARD DROMGOOLE Sr. as appears by the evidence of GEO. C. DROMGOOLE. Given under my hand this 25th day of April 1824.

Register No. 202 Teste R Turnbull CC

Brunswick County Court April 26th 1824

The above Certificate compared with the above HARTWELL & found to be Correct.

Teste R Turnbull CBC

=====

Brunswick County S ct

This is to certify that the bearer hereof TOM a free man of black colour, about fifty five years of Age five feet seven & an half Inches high has a burn on the right arm has no other apparent mark or scar on his face head or hands, recovered his freedom as appears by the within Certified copy of a Judgment of the Superior Court of Brunswick County from RICHARD COLEMAN. Given under my hand this 24th May 1824.

Register No. 203 R Turnbull CBC

A. Powell JP

Brunswick County Court May 24th 1824

The above Certificate was Compared by the Court with the person of the said TOM and found to be correct.

R Turnbull Cl

=====

Brunswick County to wit

I do hereby Certify that the bearer hereof HENRY WALKER a free man of Yellow complexion about twenty one years of Age six feet high has a scar on the Wrist of the left hand occasioned by a Cut and no other scar or mark perceivable was born free as appears from the evidence of JOHN MADDUX and by Occupation a Shoemaker. Given under my hand this 24th day of May 1824.

Register No. 204

Brunswick County Court May 24th 1824

The above Certificate was compared by the Court with the person of the said HENRY and found to be correct.

R Turnbull CBC

=====

Brunswick County S ct
This is to Certify that the bearer hereof PEGGY POMPEY a free woman of a Yellow complection about thirty five years of Age five feet five Inches high has no apparent mark or scar on her face head or hands except a small one Ring finger of the right hand, and was born free in this County as appears from the Evidence of P CLAI-BORNE. Given under my hand this 24 day of May 1824.

Register No. 205 R Turnbull CBC
Jas. Rice JP
Brunswick County Court May 24th 1824
The above Certificate was Compared by the Court with the person of the said PEGGY and found to be correct.
R Turnbull CC

=====

Brunswick County to wit
I do certify that the bearer hereof BILLY (who calls him-self BILLY CAIN) about twenty three years of age five feet six ½ In-ches high was born free and is son of LYDDIA ROBERTS one of the slaves emancipated by OWEN MYRICK dec'd by his last Will and Testament duly recorded in Brunswick County Court and has one scar only which is on the little finger of the left hand. Given under my hand this 25th day of April 1824.

Register No. 206 R Turnbull CC
C Cordle JP
Brunswick County Court May 24th 1826
The above Certificate was Compared by the Court with the said BILLY and found to be correct.
R Turnbull CC

=====

Brunswick County S ct
This is to Certify that the bearer hereof MARK a free man of Colour about Twenty four years old five feet four Inches high, has a small scar on the knuckle on the fore finger of the left hand & one also on the elbow of the left arm, and one of the Children of CATY who recovered freedom from JOHN WYCHE in the Superior Court of Law of this County at the September Term of said Court 1819. Given under my hand this 26th July 1824

Register No. 207 R Turnbull CC
Nath. Mason JP
Brunswick County Court July 26th 1824
The above Certificate was Compared with the said MARK and found to be correct.
R Turnbull CBC

=====

Brunswick County to wit
I do Certify that the bearer hereof JOHN WILLIS ROBERTS a free man of dark complexion about twenty two years of age, five feet nine Inches high has a scar on the right hand occasioned by a burn and no other scar perceivable was born free as appears from the evidence of JOHN WYCHE. Given under my hand this 23rd day of August 1824

Register No. 208 R Turnbull
Jas. Rice JP
Brunswick County Court August 24th 1824
The aboce Certificate compared & found to be correct.
R Turnbull CC

=====

Brunswick County to wit
I do Certify that the bearer hereof TEMPERANCE THOMAS a free woman of dark Complexion about five feet two & an half Inches high, twenty five years old has no scar or mark perceivable was emancipated by JAMES RAWLINGS as appears from the Instrument of writing duly recorded in the Clerks Office of said County. Given under my hand this 24th day of Augt. 1824.

Register No. 209 R Turnbull CC

Jas. Rice JP
Brunswick County Court August 26th 1824
The above Certificate compared & found to be correct.
R Turnbull CC

=====

Brunwick County to wit
I do Certify that the bearer hereof AGGY otherwise called AGGY BURG, a free woman of yellow complexion about fifty four or fifty five years of age, five feet two Inches high has a scar near the __?__ of the right ear occasioned by cutting a wire has no other scar on her face hands or arms, was emancipated by JAMES RAWLINGS as appears from the instrument of writing duly recorded in the Clerks Office of said Court. Given under my hand this 24th day of August 1824

Register No. 210 R Turnbull CC
Jas. Rice JP
Brunswick County Court August 24th 1824
The above Certificate was compared with the person of the above AGGY & found to be correct.
R Turnbull CC

=====

Brunswick County to wit

I do certify that the bearer hereof named CHARLES JONES a free man of a yellow complexion about five feet eleven Inches high about 35 years old has one ~~scar~~ two small scars on the forehead the end of the little finger on the left hand has been burnt off has no other scar or mark perceivable is one of the slaves emancipated by the last Will & Testament of BENJAMIN JONES dec'd duly recorded in the County Court of Brunswick. Given under my hand this 25th day of October 1824.

Register No. 211 R Turnbull CBC
J. Rice JP

Brunswick County October Court 25th 1824
The above certificate was compared with the person of said CHS. JONES and found to be correct.

Teste R Turnbull CC

=====

Brunswick County to wit

I do Certify that the bearer hereof PATTY (who calls herself PATTY MALONE) is a free black woman about five feet one high 36 years old has no scar or mark perceivable on head face hands or arms is one of the slaves emancipated by MICHAEL MALONE by Deed of Emancipation recorded in the County Court of Sussex as appears by the evidence of HENRY ROSE. Given under my hand this 22nd day of November 1824.

Register No. 212 Teste R Turnbull CC
Wm. ? Rice JP

Brunswick County Court November Term 1824
The above Certificate of the description of PATTY was compared with her person & found to be correct.

Teste R Turnbull CC

=======

Brunswick County to wit

I do hereby Certify that the bearer hereof DANIEL JONES a free man of dark complexion about twenty five years of age five feet Eight Inches high has a scar on the left side of the neck occasioned by a rising and no other scar or mark perceivable was emancipated by MARY JONES as appears from the Evidence of ROBERT CHEELY and by occupation a Ditcher. Given under my hand this 26th day of April 1824.

Register No. 213 R Turnbull CC
J B Mallory JP

Brunswick County March Court 1825
The above Certificate was compared with the person of the above DANIEL and found to be correct.

R Turnbull CC

=====

Brunswick County S ct

I do hereby Certify that the bearer hereof SAMUEL JONES HERCULES a free man of tawny Complexion about thirty six or seven years of age five feet 10½ Inches high has a scar on the left Eye brow & one between the left Eye and Ear & one on the under part of the right arm near the Elbow was emancipated by BENJAMIN JONES late of this County by a deed of emancipation. Given under my hand this 29th day of March 1825.

Register No. 214 R Turnbull CC
Jas. Rice JP

Brunswick County Court March 29th 1825
The above Certificate was Compared with the person of the above SAMUEL JONES HERCULES & found to be correct.

Teste R Turnbull CC

=====

Brunswick County S ct.

I do hereby Certify that the bearer hereof NANCY JONES a free woman of yellow Complexion about fifty years of age five feet eight Inches high has a scar on the right arm occasioned by whipping & several on the face was born free as appears from the Evidence of ROBERT CHEELY. Given under my hand this 29th day of March 1825.

Register No. 215 R Turnbull
Jas. Rice JP

Brunswick County Court March 29th 1825
The above Certificate was compared with the person of the above NANCY & found to be Correct.

R Turnbull CC

=====

Brunswick County to wit

I do hereby Certify that the bearer hereof SOLOMON WALKER a free Man of Colour about 50 years of age five feet six Inches high has a scar on the nose between the Eyes and another under the right eye by occupation a Carpenter was emancipated by PETER ROBINSON by Deed of emancipation recorded in the County Court of Nottoway as appears by a Certified Copy thereof.

Register No. 216 Teste R Turnbull CC
James Rice JP

Brunswick County Court March 29th 1825
The above Certificate was Compared with the person of the above SOLOMON and found to be Correct.

=====

Brunswick County to wit
I do certify that the bearer hereof JINCEY (otherwise called JINCEY MOSS) a free woman of colour about 23 years old, 5.1½ inch high has no scar or marks perceivable on her head face hands or arms and was free born as appears by the evidence of DAVID KIRKLAND is the Daughter of FED (otherwise called WAGGONER FED). Given under my hand this 26th day of June 1825.

Registered No. 217 R Turnbull
John Wyche
Brunswick County June Ct. 1825
The above certificate was compared and found to be correct.
Teste R Turnbull

=====

Brunswick County to wit
I do hereby Certify that the bearer hereof THOMAS STEWART a free man of yellow complexion five feet six inches high thirty two years old has a scar just above the cheek bone near the left eye was emancipated by the last will & testament of RICHARD STITH dec'd which has been duly recorded in the clerks office of said County and by occupation a carpenter. Given under my hand this 27th day of June 1825.

Register No. 218 R Turnbull CC

Dan'l Hicks JP
Brunswick County Court June 27th 1825
The above certificate was compared with the above THOMAS STEWART & found to be correct.
Teste R Turnbull CBC

=====

Brunswick County to wit
I do hereby certify that the bearer hereof NELLY OWEN a free woman of dark complexion 5.11 I high 32 years old has a scar on the left side of the neck occasioned by a burn & no other scar or mark perceivable was free born as appears from the evidence of ____. Given under my hand 27th day of June 1825.

Registered No. 219 R Turnbull
Benj D Chapman JP
Brunswick County Court June 27th 1825.
The above certificate was compared with the person of the said NELLY and found to be correct.
Teste R Turnbull CC

=====

Brunswick County to wit

I do hereby certify that the bearer hereof PATTY FARROW a free woman of yellow complexion 5.3 high 32 years old has no scar or mark perceivable was born free as appears from the evidence of ________ . Given under my hand the 27th day of June 1825.

Registered No. 220 Teste R Turnbull
Benj. D Chapman

Brunswick County Ct. June 27th 1825

The above certificate was compared with the person of the said PATTY & found to be correct.

Teste R Turnbull

=====

Brunswick County to wit

I do hereby certify that the bearer hereof AMOS a free man of yellow complexion, about 28 years old, 5.11 I high has a scar on the forefinger of the left hand and also a scar on each elbow recovered his freedom from DAVID HOBBS in the Superior Court of Law of Brunswick County, and by occupation a blacksmith. Given under my hand this 26th day of June 1825.

Register No. 221 R Turnbull CC
Benja. D Chapman

Brunswick County June Ct. 1825

The above certificate was compared with the person of the said AMOS & found to be correct.

Teste R Turnbull CC

=====

Brunswick County to wit

I do hereby Certify that the bearer hereof VINEY a free woman of colour about 40 years of age 5.3 high has a scar on the right arm near the elbow another on the same arm on the wrist and an other on the right side of the neck was emancipated by RICHARD M. CUNNINGHAM and was permitted to remain in this State by an order the County Court of Brunswick made July 1825. Given under my hand this 25 day of August 1825.

Registered No. 222 R Turnbull
J. Rice JP

Brunswick County Court August 22nd 1825

The above certificate was compared with the person of the said VINEY & found correct.

Teste R Turnbull CC

=====

Brunswick County to wit

I do hereby certify that the bearer hereof FLORA BERRY a free woman of colour, yellow complexion about 45 years old 5.4 high, was emancipated by THOMAS CROOK by deed of emancipation as appears by the evidence of CHARLES TUCKER has no scar or mark perceivable on her head, face hands or arms. Given under my hand the 22nd day of August 1825.

Registered No. 223 R Turnbull CC
J. Rice JP

Brunswick County August Court 1825

The above certificate was compared with the person of said FLORA BERRY and found to be correct.

Teste R Turnbull CC

=====

Brunswick County to wit

I do hereby certify that the bearer hereof BETSEY LAWSON a free woman of colour about 32 years of age, five feet eight inches high was born free in this County as appears by the evidence of CHARLES TUCKER has no scar or mark perceivable on her head face hands or arms. Given under my hand the 22nd day of August 1825.

Registered No. 224 Teste R Turnbull
Js. Rice JP

Brunswick County August Court 1825

The above certificate was compared with the person of said BETSEY LAWSON and found to be correct.

Teste R Turnbull

=====

Brunswick County S ct

I do hereby Certify that the bearer hereof DANIEL JAMES a free man of yellow Complexion about fifty two years old five feet seven or eight Inches high has a small scar or mark below the left eye no other mark or scar perceivable on his head face hands or arms is one of the slaves emancipated by EDWD. DROMGOOLE by deed of emancipation recorded in the County Court of Brunswick. Given under my hand this 26th day of September 1825.

Register No. 224 R Turnbull CC
Nathl. E. Malry JP

Brunswick County September 26th 1825

The above Certificate was Compared with the person of the said DANIEL JAMES & found to be correct.

R Turnbull CC

=====

Brunswick County to wit
I do hereby Certify that the bearer hereof PATSEY alias PATSEY GRAIN a free woman of Colour of black Complexion about twenty seven years old five feet four Inches high has no scar perceivable on her head face hands or arms and was free born in this County. Given under my hand this 26th day of September 1825

Register No. 225 R Turnbull CC
Nathl. E Malry JP
Brunswick County September 26th 1825.
The above Certificate was compared with the person of the above PATSY & found to be correct.
Teste R Turnbull CC

=====

Brunswick County to wit
I do hereby Certify that the bearer hereof LIZZY ROBERTS a free woman of colour yellow Complexion about twenty three years old five feet three Inches high has no apparent scar or mark on her head face hands or arms was born free in this County. Given under my hand this 26th day of September 1825.

Register No. 226 R Turnbull CC
Nathl. E. Malry JP
Brunswick County September 26th 1825
The above Certificate was compared with the person of the above LIZZY and found to be correct.
Teste R Turnbull CC

=====

Brunswick County to wit
I do hereby Certify that the bearer hereof POLLY ROBERTS a free woman of yellow complexion about nineteen years old five feet three Inches high has no apparent scar or mark on her head face hands or arms was born free in this County. Given under my hand this 26th day of September 1825.

Register No. 227 R Turnbull CC
Nathl. E Malry JP
Brunswick County September 26th 1825
The above Certificate was compared with the person of the above POLLY & found to be correct.
Teste R Turnbull CC

=====

Brunswick County S ct.

I do hereby Certify that the bearer hereof ROBERT MERRITT a free man of colour black Complexion five feet four Inches high, about forty five years old, has a mark on the back of the right hand, another on the wrist of said hand also another on the nose a little to the side next to the left eye (the scars small ones) is one of the slaves emancipated by HENRY MERRITT by Deed of emancipation duly recorded in the Clerks Office of the County Court of Brunswick. Given under my hand this 26th day of September 1825.

Register No. 228 R Turnbull CC
Nathl. E Malry JP

Brunswick County September 26th 1825

The above Certificate was compared with the above ROBERT MERITT & found to be correct.

Teste R Turnbull CC

=====

Brunswick County to wit

I do hereby certify that the bearer hereof GEORGE ANDERSON SEWARD a free man of dark complexion about 6 feet high 21 years old one scar on the right arm several small scars on the left arm and one on the right shoulder, all of which were occasioned by burns was born free as appears from the Evidence of THOMAS SMITH. Given under my hand this 24 day of October 1825.

Registered No. 229 R Turnbull CC
Rich'd. Fletcher JP

Brunswick County October Court 1825

The above certificate was compared with the person of said A. SEWARD and found to be correct.

Teste R Turnbull

=====

Brunswick County to wit

I do hereby certify that the bearer hereof MIKE alias MIKE ADKINS, a free man of black complection, about 46 years of age 5 feet 6 inches high has no apparent mark or scar on head, face, hands, or arms, by occupation a ditcher was emancipated by the last Will and Testament, of LUCY ADKINS duly recorded in Sussex County Court as appears by and attested copy of thereof. Given under my hand this 23rd day of October.

Registered No. 230 R Turnbull
Rich'd. Fletcher JP

Brunswick County Court October 1825

The above certificate was compared by the Court with the person of said MIKE ADKINS and found to be correct.

Teste R Turnbull

=====

Brunswick County to wit
I do hereby certify that the bearer hereof BOB TUCKER a free man of yellow complexion about 35 years old 5.9 inches high long bushy hair has no scar perceivable on his head face hands or arms perceivable and emancipated by JOHN TUCKER by Deed of emancipation this day recorded in Brunswick County Court. Given under my hand this 26 December 1825

Register No. 231 R Turnbull
Js. Rice JP

Brunswick County December Court 1825
The above certificate was compared with the person of said BOB & found to be correct.

Teste R Turnbull

=====

Brunswick County to wit
I do hereby Certify that the bearer hereof EDMUND MATHEWS a free man of yellow complexion about thirty eight years old about five feet ten or Eleven Inches high has a small scar on the inside of his left wrist & few small ones on each arm & no other scar or mark on his head or hands perceivable who it appears was born free as appears from a former Certificate. Given under my hand this 23rd day of January 1826.

Register No. 232 R Turnbull CC
John Tucker JP

Brunswick County Court January 23rd 1826
This Certificate was compared with the person of the above EDMUND & found to be correct.

Teste R Turnbull CBC

=====

Brunswick County to wit
I do hereby certify that the bearer hereof SUSAN NEUSUM (wife of AARON NEUSUM) a free bright mulatto woman 5 feet 4 inches high about 27 years old was born free as appears by the evidence of BENJ. D CHAPMAN has long bushy hair no apparent scar on her head face hands or arms. Given under my hand this 23 January 1826.

Register No. 233 Teste R Turnbull
F W Greene JP

Brunswick County Jany. Court 1826
The above certificate was compared by the Court with the person of said SUSAN & found to be correct.

Teste R Turnbull Clk

=====

Brunswick County to wit
I do hereby certify that the bearer hereof AARON NEUSUM, a dark brown mulatto man who it appears from a certificate of the clerk of the Hustings Court of Petersburg was born free and raised in the County of Greensville about 52 years old 5 feet 10 inches high by occupation a planter has no mark or scar on his head face hands or arms worth noticing. Given under my hand 23rd of January 1826.

Registered No. 234 R Turnbull C B

Brunswick County Jany. Ct. 1826.
The above certificate compared by the Court & found to be correct.
Teste R Turnbull Ck

=====

Brunswick County to wit
This is to Certify that the bearer hereof SAMUEL WALKER a free man yellow complexion five feet six Inches high, about nineteen years old has a scar on the forefinger of the left hand & another on the Middle finger of the same hand was born free in this County as appears from the Evidence of ISHAM TROTTER. Given under my hand the 27th day of February 1826.

Register No. 235 Teste R Turnbull CC
John Wyche

Brunswick County Court February 27th 1826
The above Certificate was compared with the above SAMUEL WALKER & found to be correct.
Teste R Turnbull CC

=====

Brunswick County to wit
I do Certify that the bearer hereof ISAAC THOMAS a free coloured man about thirty four years of age five Feet Eight & an half Inches high has a scar on the right side of head two on the forehead & one on knuckles of the ring finger that joins the left hand and is one of the slaves emancipated by OWEN MYRICK by his last will and Testament duly recorded in the County Court of Brunswick as appears by the Evidence of JOHN WYCHE. Given under my hand the 26th day of June 1826.

Register No. 236 Teste R Turnbull CC

Edw'd. C Smith JP

Brunswick County Court June 26th 1826
The above Certificate was compared by the court with the person of the said ISAAC THOMAS & found to be correct.
Teste R Turnbull CC

=====

Brunswick County to wit

I do hereby certify that the bearer hereof ADAM ABRAM, a free man of dark complexion about 54 years of age 5 F 1½ I high has a scar just below the thumb of the right hand was emancipated by EDWARD DROMGOOLE SR. of this County by Deed of Emancipation duly recorded in the Court of this County. Given under my hand this 24th July 1826.

Registered No. 237 R Turnbull Clk.
F W Greene JP

Brunswick County July Court 1826

The above certificate was compared by the Court with the person & said ADAM & found to be correct.

Teste R Turnbull CC

=====

Brunswick County to wit

I do hereby Certify that the bearer hereof WINNEY HERCULES a bright mulatto aged about thirty five years of age five feet one Inch high bright complexion a scar under the corner of her right eye by occupation a spinster, has been duly registered in the Clerks Office of Dinwiddie County and was allowed to remain in this State by an Order of the said County Court of Dinwiddie as appears by a Copy of the order of the said Court. Given under my hand this 24th of July 1826.

Register No. 238 Teste R Turnbull CC
John Wyche JP

Brunswick County July Court 1826

The above Certificate was Compared by this Court with the person of the above WINNEY and found to be Correct.

Teste R Turnbull CBC

=====

Brunswick County to wit

I do hereby Certify that the bearer hereof CATO GOODRICH a free man of Colour about forty nine years of age five feet six & an half Inches high light Complexion has a mole under the left nostril, was emancipated by RICHARD M CUNNINGHAM by deed of emancipation duly recorded in this Court and was allowed to remain in this State by an order of the County Court of Brunswick is duly registered in my Office on this 28th day of August 1826.

Register No. 239 Teste R Turnbull CC
F W Green JP

Brunswick County Court August 28th 1826

The above Certificate was Compared with the person of the above CATO & found to be Correct.

Teste R Turnbull CC

=====

Brunswick County Sc
I do hereby Certify that the bearer hereof VINEY GOODRICH a free woman of Colour about forty one years of age five feet three Inches high has a scar on the right arm near the elbow another on the wrist of the same arm & one on the wright side of neck was emancipated by RICHARD M CUNNINGHAM by deed of emancipation duly recorded in this Court and was permitted to remain in this State by an order of Court made July 1825 is duly registered in my office on this 28th day of August 1826.

Register No. 240 Teste R Turnbull CC
F W Green JP
Brunswick County Court August 28th 1826
The above Certificate was compared with the person of the above VINEY & found to be correct.
Teste R Turnbull CC

=====

Brunswick County to wit
I do hereby Certify that the bearer hereof CREACY MALONE a free girl of black complexion about five feet one Inch high, seventeen years old has a scar on the ring finger of the right hand, was free in this County as appears by the Evidence of HENRY ROSE and is duly registered in my office on this 29th of August 1826.

Register No. 241 Teste R Turnbull CC
John Wyche JP
Brunswick County Court August 29th 1826
The above Certificate was compared with the above CREACY and found to be correct.
Teste R Turnbull CC

=====

Brunswick County to wit
This is to certify that the bearer hereof DOSTIN POMPEY a a free man of yellow complexion about Twenty five years old six feet high has a scar on the right arm and one on the middle finger of the right hand and by occupation a Carpenter was born free in this County as appears by the Evidence of PHIL CLAIBORNE is duly registered in my office.

No. 242

Brunswick County Court September 23rd 1826
The above Certificate was compared with the said DOSTIN POMPEY & found to be correct.
Teste R Turnbull CC

=====

Brunswick County to wit
I Certify that the bearer hereof ABRAM ROBERTS a free man of dark complexion about forty nine years of age five feet nine & an half Inches high a scar on the right Cheek & another on the inside of the left hand also a large scar on the forehead rather over the left eye & no other scar or mark perceivable was emancipated by OWEN MYRICK as appears from a former Certificate produced by the said ABRAM ROBERTS. Given under my hand this 22nd day of September 1823.

Register No. 243 Teste R Turnbull CC
John Tucker JP
Brunswick County Court September 25th 1826
This Certificate was Compared with the person of the above ABRAM ROBERTS & found to be correct.
Teste R Turnbull CC

=====

Brunswick County to wit
I do hereby certify that the bearer hereof PRISCILLA MITCHELL a free woman of yellow complexion 5"5 inches high 21 years old, was born free in this County as appears by the Evidence of JOHN WYCHE and is duly registered in my office on this 25 day of September 1826.
Register No. 244 Teste R Turnbull CC
Signed John Tucker JP
Brunswick County September Court 1826
The above certificate of the description of PRISCILLA MITCHELL was compared by the Court with the person and found to be correct.
Teste R Turnbull

=====

Brunswick County to wit
I do Certify that the bearer hereof KINCHIN BOWSER a free man of yellow Complexion about five feet three Inches high thirty years of age was born free as appears from the Evidence of JOHN D WILKINS and has no scars or marks perceivable and by Occupation a Ditcher. Given under my hand this 26th day of June 1826.

Register No. 245 Teste R Turnbull
John Wyche
Brunswick County Court June 26th 1826
The above Certificate was Compared with the person of the above KINCHIN BOWSER and found to be Correct.
Teste R Turnbull CC

=====

Brunswick County to wit

The Bearer hereof BETSEY ROBERTS a free woman of colour of a yellow complexion about five feet two & half Inches high about fift years of age has a scar on the left hand & wrist which was occasione by a cut was born free in this County is duly registered in my office Given under my hand this 25th day of October 1826.

Register No. 246 Teste R Turnbull CC
Jas. Rice JP

Brunswick County Court November 29th 1826
The above Certificate was Compared with the person of the above & found to be Correct.

R Turnbull CC

=====

Brunswick County S c

I do hereby certify that the bearer hereof MATTHEW GRAIN a free man of a yellow complexion about 23 years old 6 feet 6 inches high has a small scar on the right arm just above the wrist was born free as appears from the evidence of R H H WALLTON and by occupation a ditcher. Given under my hand this 25th September 1826.

Register No. 247 Teste R Turnbull
Signed John Tucker JP

Brunswick County Court September 1826
The above certificate was compared by the Court with the person of the said MATTHEW GRAIN & found to be correct.

Teste R Turnbull CC

=====

Brunswick County to wit

I do hereby certify that the bearer hereof SIDDY STEWART a free woman of yellow complexion about 21 or 23 years of age five feet high has no scar or mark perceivable, is the daughter of MOLLY STEW-ART a free woman as appears from the evidence of PHIL CLAIBORNE. Given under my hand this 26th day of February 1827.

Register No. 248 Teste R Turnbull
Signed John Wyche JP

Brunswick County February 26th 1827
The above certificate was compared with the person of above SIDDY STEWART and found to be correct.

Teste R Turnbull

=====

Brunswick County to wit

I do hereby certify that the bearer hereof MOLLY STEWART a free woman of color about 5 feet 2½ Inches high about 55 years of age has a scar on the left cheek and another on the right Jawline and of a yellow complexion was born free as appears from the evidence of PHIL CLAIBORNE. Given under my hand this 26th day of February 18 1827.

Registered No. 249 Teste R Turnbull CC
John Wyche JP

Brunswick County February Court 1827
The above certificate was compared with the person of said MOLLY and found to be correct.

Teste R Turnbull CC

=====

(Note: The next three Registers are incorrectly numbered but are copied as they appear in the book.)

Brunswick County to wit

I do hereby Certify that the bearer hereof JIM EASTER a free man of black of black (sic) complexion six feet high Twenty three years of age has a scar on the breast & another in the palm of the left hand & one other scar on the wright wrist was born (sic) as appears from the Evidence of RICHARD FLETCHER and by occupation a Ditcher, and was duly registered in my office. Given under my hand this 26th day of February 1827.

Register No. 450 (sic) R Turnbull CC
John Wyche JP

Brunswick County Court February 26th 1827
The above Certificate was Compared with the person of the above JIM EASTER & found to be Correct.

Teste R Turnbull CC

=====

Brunswick County to wit

I do hereby Certify that the bearer hereof WESTLY CAIN a free man of Colour about twenty one years of age five feet six Inches high has no scar or mark perceivable was born free & is by occupation a Ditcher is duly registered in my office on this 28th day of August 1826.

Register No. 451 (sic) Teste R Turnbull CC
F. W. Green JP

Brunswick County Court August Term 1826
The above Certificate was compared with the above WESTLY CAIN and found to be Correct.

Teste R Turnbull CC

====

Brunswick County to wit
I do hereby Certify that the bearer hereof ALFRED HARRISON a free man of yellow complexion about five feet nine inches high twenty two years old has a scar on the face near the right temple & one on the left arm near the wrist occasioned by Cuts was born free as appears by the Evidence of PHIL CLAIBORNE and by Occupation a sawyer. Given under my hand this 26th day of February 1827.

Register No. 452 (sic) R Turnbull
John Wyche JP
Brunswick County Court February 26th 1827
The above Certificate was Compared with the said ALFRED HARRISON & found to be Correct.
Teste R Turnbull CC

=====

Brunswick County to wit
I do hereby Certify that the bearer hereof OSBORN BOIKEN (VICK) a free man of Dark Complexion about Twenty three years of age five feet five Inches high has no scars or marks perceivable was born free as appears from the Evidence of JAMES RICE. Given under my hand this 22nd day of May 1826.

Register No. 253 R Turnbull CC
James Rice JP
Brunswick County Court May 22nd 1826
The above Certificate was compared with the person of the said BOIKEN & found to be correct.
Teste R Turnbull CC

=====

Brunswick County to wit
I do Certify that the bearer hereof MACLIN SEWARD a free man of Colour of dark Complexion five feet six & a half Inches high twenty years old has a scar on the right wrist occasioned by a burn was born free as appears from the evidence of JAMES J HARRISON. Given under my hand this 27th day of November 1826.
Register No. 254 R Turnbull CC
J B Mallory JP
Brunswick County Court July 23rd 1827
The above Certificate was compared with the person of the above MACLIN SEWARD & found to be correct.
Teste R Turnbull CC

=====

Brunswick County to wit
I do Certify that the bearer hereof ALLEN CAIN a free man of Colour dark Complexion five feet 10½ Inches hightwenty years of age has a scar on the right arm & one on the left arm was born free as appears from the evidence of PHIL CLAIBORNE & by occupation a Ditcher & is duly registered in my office on the 29th day of May 1827.

Register No. 255 R Turnbull CC
J B Mallory JP

Brunswick County Court July 23rd 1827
The above Certificate was Compared with the person of the above ALLEN CAIN & found to be Correct.
Teste R Turnbull CC

=====

Brunswick County to wit
I do hereby Certify that the bearer hereof DELILAH SEWARD a free woman of Colour yellow complexion nineteen years of age five feet 3½ Inches high has no scar or mark perceivable was born free as appears from the evidence of JAMES J HARRISON and is duly registered in my office this 23rd day of July 1827.

Register No. 255 R Turnbull CC
J B Mallory JP
Brunswick County Court July 23rd 1827
The above Certificate was Compared with the person of the above DELILAH & found to be Correct.
Teste R Turnbull CC

=====

Brunswick County to wit
I do hereby Certify that the bearer hereof GEORGE EASTER a free man of dark Complexion five feet 8 Inches high twenty three years of age was born free as appears by the Evidence of PHIL CLAIBORNE & by Occupation a Ditcher & is duly registered in my office this 29th day of May 1827.
Register No. 256 R Turnbull
Jas. Rice JP
Brunswick County Court August 27th 1827
The above Certificate was Compared with the above GEORGE EASTER & found to be correct.
R Turnbull CC

=====

Brunswick County to wit
I do hereby Certify that the bearer hereof JOHN MASON a free man of dark Complexion 5 feet 5 Inches high 43 years old several scars on the right hand & one on the right temple occasioned by a cut of a machine & one scar on the lip was emancipated by JOHN MASON as appears from the evidence of PHIL CLAIBORNE & by Occupation a Ditcher. Given under my hand this 29th day of May 1827 and is duly registered in my office.

Register No. 257 R Turnbull CC
J W Green JP
Brunswick County Court August 1827
The above Certificate was Compared with the person of the above JOHN MASON & found to be Correct.
Teste R Turnbull CC

=====

Brunswick County to wit
I do hereby certify that the bearer hereof JEFF ADKINS six feet high, aged twenty nine, dark complexioned, was born free as appears by the evidence of FREDERICK W. GREENE & is duly registered in my office this 28th day of August 1827.

Register No. 258 R Turnbull CC
J. Rice JP
Brunswick County Court August 28th 1827
The above certificate was compared with the person of the said JEFF ADKINS & found to be correct.
Teste R Turnbull

=====

Brunswick County to wit
This is to Certify that the bearer hereof MOSES a black man about 6 feet high 45 or 46 years old has a scar under the eye & was emancipated by PETER ROBINSON Exor of BENJAMIN JONES who was Exor of WM WALKER as will appear by a deed of emancipation recorded in the office of Brunswick County Court. Given under my hand the 13th day of Feby 1828.

Register No. 259 R Turnbull CC
James Rice JP
Brunswick County Court February 25th 1828
The above certificate was compared with the person of the said MOSES & found to be correct.
Teste R Turnbull CC

=====

Brunswick County to wit
I do hereby certify that the bearer hereof ROBERT CROOK a mulatto man, about forty years of age six feet & half inch high by occupation a butcher with the fore finger of his left hand discolated, was born free as appears by the evidence of GEORGE W TUCKER is duly registered in my office this 25th day of February 1828.

Register No. 260 Teste R Turnbull CC
Isham Trotter JP
Brunswick County Court February 25th 1828
The above certificate was compared with the person of the above RO-ROBERT CROOK & found to be correct.
Teste R Turnbull CC

=====

Brunswick County to wit
I do hereby Certify that JANE WALKER the bearer hereof a free mulatto woman about forty five years of age five feet one Inch high has a scar on the left hand & was emancipated by a deed from JOSEPH CROOK & is duly registered in my office this 25th day of February 1828.

Register No. 261 Teste R Turnbull CC
Isham Trotter JP
Brunswick County Court February 25th 1828
The above Certificate was compared with the person of the above JANE WALKER & found to be correct.
Teste R Turnbull CC

=====

Brunswick County to wit
I do hereby Certify that the bearer hereof LEWIS HENRY a free man of Colour about fifty two years of age five feet three Inches & an half high of a black complexion has a scar on the left ear & another between the wrist & nuckle of the thumb on the left hand was emancipated by Deed of emancipation from JOHN BREWER duly recorded in the Court of said County. Given under my hand this 26th day of November 1827.

Register No. 262 R Turnbull CC
Wm. Gholson JP
Brunswick County Court March 24th 1828
The above Certificate was compared with the person of the above HENRY & found to be correct.
Teste R Turnbull CC

=====

Brunswick County to wit

I do hereby certify that the bearer hereof NANCY HARRISON a free woman of light complexion about forty five years of age, five feet high was born free as appears by the evidence of JAMES J.HARRISON and is duly registered in my office on the 24th day of March AD 1828.

Register No. 262 (sic) R Turnbull CC
Js. Rice JP

Brunswick County Court March 24th 1828

The above certificate was compared with the person of the above NANCY HARRISON & found to be correct.

Teste R Turnbull CC

=====

Brunswick County to wit

I do hereby certify that the bearer hereof HANNAH HARRISON, a free woman of light complexion, about nineteen years of age, four feet eleven and an half inches high, was born free as appears by the evidence of JAMES J. HARRISON and is duly registered in my office on the 24th day of March AD 1828.

Register No. 263 R Turnbull CC
Js. Rice JP

Brunswick County Court March 24th 1828

The above certificate was compared with the person of the above HANNAH HARRISON & found to be correct.

Teste R Turnbull CC

=====

Brunswick County to wit

I do hereby certify that the bearer hereof MARIA JONES a free woman of colour, light complexion, five feet, three & an half inches high, sixty years of age, has no scar perceivable & was emancipated as appears by a deed of record in the Office of Brunswick County Court from BENJAMIN JONES & is duly registered in my Office this 3th day of February 1828.

Register No. 264 R Turnbull CC
Js. Rice JP

Brunswick County Court March 24th 1828

The above certificate was compared with the person of the above MARIA JONES & found to be correct.

R Turnbull CC

=====

Brunswick County to wit
I do hereby certify that the bearer hereof ABEDNIGO, light complexion, 58 years of age, five feet & a half inches high, has no perceivable scar, has lost his foreteeth & was emancipated by a deed from MARY JONES recorded in the Clerks Office of this Court. Given under my hand this 25th day of February 1828.

Register No. 265 R Turnbull CC
Js. Rice JP

Brunswick County Court March 25th 1828
The above certificate was compared with the person of the above ABEDNIGO & found to be correct.

Teste R Turnbull CC

=====

Brunswick County to wit
I do certify that the bearer hereof LIZZY JONES a free woman of colour, light complexion, five feet two and an half inches high, twenty three years of age, has no scar perceivable & was born free as appears by the evidence of JOHN H. HARWELL & is duly registered in my Office this 13th day of February 1828.

Register No. 266 R Turnbull CC

Brunswick County Court March 25th 1828
The above certificate was compared with the person of the above LIZZY JONES & found to be correct.

Teste R Turnbull CC

=====

Brunswick County to wit
I do hereby certify that the bearer hereof CELIA OWEN a free woman of colour, about twenty two years of age, of a yellow complexion, five feet, two inches high, with a scar on the left arm occasioned by a burn, was born free as appears by the evidence of JOHN M. LUNDIE and is registered in my Office this 25th day of March 1828.

Register No. 267 R Turnbull CC
Js. Rice JP

Brunswick County Court March 25th 1828
The above certificate was compared with the person of the above CELIA OWEN & found to be correct.

R Turnbull CC

=====

Brunswick County to wit

I do hereby certify that the bearer hereof SALLY JONES a free woman of colour black complexion five feet & an half inch high twenty five years old was born free as appears by the evidence of JNO. H. HARWELL and is duly registered in my Office. Given under my hands this 25th day of March 1828.

Register No. 268 R Turnbull CC
Js. Rice JP

Brunswick County Court March 26th 1828
The above certificate was compared with the person of the above SALLY & found to be correct.

R Turnbull CC

=====

Brunswick County to wit

I do hereby certify that the bearer hereof TURNER BYNAM HARRISON, a free boy of colour, aged about twenty years, five feet, six inches and a quarter in height, of a light complexion, was born free as appears by the evidence of DAVID KIRKLAND and is duly registered in my office this 25th day of March 1828.

Register No. 269 R Turnbull CC
Js. Rice JP

Brunswick County Court, March 26th 1828
The above certificate was compared with the person of the above TURNER BYNAM HARRISON & found to be correct.

Teste R Turnbull CC

=====

Brunswick County to wit

I do hereby certify that the bearer hereof ANTHONY SMITH a free man of a yellow complexion, aged about forty six years, five feet six inches high has a scar on the underpart of the left arm between the wrist and elbow, was born free as appears by the evidence of MARY BROWN and is duly registered in my Office this 27th day of March 1818.

Register No. 270 R Turnbull CC
Js. Rice JP

Brunswick County Court, March 27th 1828
The above certificate was compared with the person of the above ANTHONY SMITH & found to be correct.

R Turnbull CC

=====

Brunswick County to wit
I do Certify that MICHAEL ADKINS a free man of colour about twenty seven years of age five feet Eleven & an half Inches high has no scars or marks perceivable was born free as appears from the evidence of FREDERICK W. GREEN and by Occupation a Ditcher and is duly registered in my office this 27th day of August 1827.

Register No. 271 R Turnbull CC
James Rice JP
Brunswick County Court August 27th 1828
The above Certificate was compared with the person of the above MICHAEL ADKINS & found to be correct.
Teste R Turnbull CC

=====

Brunswick County to wit
I do hereby certify that the bearer hereof PEGGY MALONE a free woman of a black complexion aged twenty four years five feet one inch and a quarter in height was emancipated by MICHAEL MALONE and is duly registered in my office on the 28th day of July AD 1828.

Register No. 272 R Turnbull CC
Wm H Worthington
Brunswick County Court July 28th 1828
The above certificate was compared with the person of the above PEGGY MALONE & found to be correct.
Teste R Turnbull CC

=====

Brunswick County to wit
I do hereby (sic) that the bearer hereof ISAAC a free man of a yellowish complexion about sixty years of age, about five feet three inches high a small scar on the back of the left hand opposite the forefinger & a very small scar or mark on the nose between the eyes. Appears to have been emancipated by JOHN SEWARD as appears by the evidence of _______________ and is duly registered in my Office. Given under my hand this 28th day of July 1828.

Register No. 273 R Turnbull CC
Js. Rice
Brunswick County Court 28 July 1828

The above certificate was compared with the person of the above ISAAC and found to be correct.
Teste R Turnbull CC

=====

Brunswick County to wit
I do hereby certify that the bearer hereof WASHINGTON WOOD LEY five feet nine inches & a quarter high aged twenty one years ligh complexion with a scar on the left hand was set free as appears by a deed of emancipation from EDWARD DRUMGOOL senior & is duly registere in my Office this 28th day of August 1827.

Register No. 274
Js. Rice
Brunswick County Court 28th August 18th August (sic) 1827
The above certificate was compared with the person of the above WASHINGTON WOODLEY & found to be correct.
R Turnbull CC

=====

Brunswick County to wit
I do hereby certify that the bearer hereof NANCY SEWARD a free woman of dark complexion about thirty five years of agefive feet and five eights of an inch in height with only one small visable scar that being found on the right arm near the elbow was born free as appears by the record from my Office this 28th day of July 1828.

Wm H Worthington
Register No. 275 R Turnbull CC
Brunswick County Court 28th July 1828
The above certificate was compared with the person of the above NANCY SEWARD & found to be correct.
Teste R Turnbull CBC

=====

Brunswick County to wit
I do hereby certify that the bearer hereof BECKY JACKSON a free woman of light complexion five feet five Inches and a half high with a scar on the inside of the left thumb no other visable mark aged about twenty eight years was born free as appears by the evidence of W. ALLAN. Given under my hand this 25th day of August 1828.

Register No. 276 R Turnbull CBC
D Hicks
Brunswick County August 25th 1828
The above certificate was compared with the person of the above BECK JACKSON and found to be correct.
Teste R Turnbull CBC

=====

Brunswick County to wit
I do hereby certify that the bearer hereof EASTER ROBERTS a free woman of dark complexion five feet six and a half Inches high with a small mark on the right Thumb aged about twenty eight years. Born free as appears by the evidence of GEORGE C DRUMGOOL. Given under my hand this 25th day of August 1828.

Register No. 276 (sic) R Turnbull CBC
E C Smith JP
Brunswick County Court August 25th 1828
The above certificate was compared with the person of the above EASTER ROBERTS and found to be correct.
Teste R Turnbull CBC

=====

Brunswick County to Wit
I do hereby certify that the bearer hereof VIOLET WOODLEY a free Woman of light complexion five feet one inch high no visable scar aged about forty four years and emancipated as appears by the evidence of GEORGE C DRUMGOOL. Given under my hand this 25th day of August 1828

Register No. 277 R Turnbull CBC
E C Smith JP
Brunswick County County (sic) August 25th 1828
The above certificate was compared with the person of the above VIOLET WOODLEY & found to be correct.
Teste R Turnbull CBC

=====

Brunswick County to Wit
I do hereby certify that the bearer hereof OTHA MERRITT a free woman of light complexion five feet and a half Inch high one long scar under the left arm aged twenty one years. Born free as appears by the evidence of WM. ALLAN. Given under my hand this 25th day of August 1828

Register No. 278 R Turnbull CBC
D Hicks JP

=====

Brunswick County to Wit
I do hereby certify that the bearer hereof VIOLET GRAIN a free woman of light Complexion five feet one & five / 8 Inches high no visable scar aged about twenty five years. Born free as appears by the evidence of WM ALLAN. Given under my hand this 25th day of August 1828

Register No. 279 R Turnbull CBC
D Hicks JP

Brunswick County Court August 25th 1828
The above certificate was compared with the person of VIOLET GRAIN and found to be correct.
Teste R Turnbull CBC

=====

Brunswick County to Wit
I do hereby certify that the bearer hereof LUCY MERRITT a free woman of dark complexion five feet eight Inches high only one visable scar that being found on the back of her left hand aged about twenty five years. She appears to have been born free by the evidence of WM ALLEN. Given under my hand this 25th day of August 1828.

Register No. 290 R Turnbull CBC
D. Hicks JP
Brunswick County Court August 25th 1828
The above certificate was compared with the person of the above LUCY MERRITT and found to be correct.
Teste R Turnbull CBC

=====

Brunswick County to Wit
I do hereby certify that the bearer hereof ELIZA CAIN a free woman of dark complexion five feet two Inches high stutters badly aged about twenty five years. Born free as appears by the evidence of RICHARD FLETCHER. Given under my hand this 25th day of Augus 1828

Register No. 281 R Turnbull CBC
D Hicks JP
Brunswick County Court August 25th 1828
The above certificate was compared with the person of the above ELIZA CAIN & found to be correct.
Teste R Turnbull CBC

=====

Brunswick County to wit

I do hereby certify that the bearer hereof CHARLES MERRITT a free man of dark complexion 5 feet eight Inches high forty eight years of age one scar on the left wrist burned Was emancipated by HENRY MERRITT by Deed of Record in this Court and by Occupation Farmer & is duly registered in my Office. Given under my hand this 29th day of May 1827

Registered No. 282 R Turnbull CC
B D Chapman

Brunswick County Court May 29th 1828
The above certificate was compared with the person of the above CHARLES MERRITT and found to be correct.

Teste R Turnbull CC

=====

Brunswick County to Wit

I do hereby certify that the bearer hereof FANNY MERRITT a free woman of dark complexion five feet two & a half inches high one scar behind her left ear aged about twenty two years born free as appears by the evidence of WM ALLAN. Given under my hand this 25th day of August 1828

Register No. 283 R Turnbull CBC
D Hicks JP

Brunswick County Court August 26th 1828
The above certificate was compared with the person of the above FANNY MERRITT and found to be correct.

Teste R Turnbull CBC

=====

Brunswick County to Wit

I do hereby certify that the bearer hereof ROBERT ROBERTS a free man of colour about fifty eight years of age light complexion the little finger on the left hand crooked five feet seven inches & a half high was emancipated by the last will and testament of OWEN MYRICK dec'd of record in this Office of Brunswick County Court. Given under my hand this 26th day of August AD 1828

Register No. 284 R Turnbull CC
D Hicks JP

Brunswick County Court August 26th 1828
The above certificate was compared with the person of the above ROBERT ROBERTS and found to be correct.

Teste R Turnbull CBC

=====

Brunswick County to wit
I do hereby certify that the bearer hereof WYATT STEWART a free man of colour, dark complexion, five feet nine & a half inches high twenty one years Old has a scar on his right eye brow occasioned by a cut, was born free as appears by the evidence of JOHN WYCHE & R. H. H. WALLTON & by occupation a ditcher & is duly registered in my Office this 22nd day of September 1828

Register No. 285 R Turnbull CC
Benjamin D Chapman JP
Brunswick County Court September 22nd 1828
The above certificate was compared with the person of the above WYATT STEWART & found to be correct.
Teste R Turnbull CC

=====

Brunswick County to wit
I do hereby certify that HANSAL HARRISON the bearer hereof, a free man of yellow Complexion, about twenty two years of age five feet eight and a quarter inches high, one scar on the top of his head a small one over his right eye, and one in his forehead, was born free as appears by the evidence of PASCAL HICKS and JOSEPH SEWARD. Given under my hand this 27th day of October 1828

Register No. 286 R Turnbull CC
John Wyche JP
Brunswick County Court October 27th 1828
The above certificate was compared with the person of the above HANSEL HARRISON & found to be correct
Teste R Turnbull CC

=====

Brunswick County to wit
I do certify that the bearer hereof, BILLY (who calls himself BILLY CAIN) about twenty seven years old, five feet six & an half inches high, was born free, and is son of LYDDIA ROBERTS, one of the slaves emancipated by OWEN MYRICK dec'd by his last Will & Testament duly recorded in Brunswick County Court and has a scar on the fore finger of the left hand. Given under my hand this 28th day of October 1828.

Register No. 287 R Turnbull CC
John Wyche
Brunswick County Court October 28th 1828
The above Certificate was compared with the person of the above BILLY CAIN and found to be correct.
Teste R Turnbull CC

=====

Brunswick County to wit
I do hereby certify that CHARLES ROBERTS a free man of a yellow complexion, five feet eight inches high, has a scar on his forehead, and one immediately, under his left ear occasioned by burns, about twenty five years of age, and was born free as appears by the evidence of JOHN WYCHE. Given under my hand this 24th day of November 1828

Register No. 288 R Turnbull CC
F W Green JP
Brunswick County Court November 24th 1828
The above certificate was compared with the person of the above CHARLES ROBERTS and found to be correct

=====

Brunswick County to wit
I do hereby Certify that LOUIS COUSINS, the bearer hereof a free man of dark complexion about five feet five & an half Inches high has a small scar in his forehead with none other visable about twenty eight years of age and was borne free as appears by the Evidence of JAMES E WEBB. Given under my hand this 24th day of November 1828

Register No. 289 R Turnbull CC
Burwell B Wilkes JP
Brunswick County Court November 24th 1828
The above Certificate was compared with the person of the above LEWIS COUSINS & found to be correct.
Teste R Turnbull CC

=====

Brunswick County to wit
I do hereby Certify that JOSHUA COUSINS the bearer hereof a free man of yellow complexion five feet five Inches high has a small scar on his left arm about twenty four years of age was born free as appears from the Evidence of JAMES E. WEBB. Given under my hand this 24th day of November 1828

Register No. 290 R Turnbull CC
B B Wilkes JP
Brunswick County Court November 24th 1828
The above certificate was compared with the person of the above JOSHUA COUSINS & found to be correct.
Teste R Turnbull CC

=====

Brunswick County Sc

I do hereby certify that the bearer hereof ISAAC a free man of dark complexion five feet seven and a half inches high about forty six years of age has a small scar on the top of his right hand and the end of his middle finger on the same hand seems to have been broken, and who is it appears one of the slaves emancipated by the last will and testament of GRAY EDMUNDS dec'd. Given under my hand this 22nd day of December 1828.

Register No. 291 R Turnbull CC
E C Smith

Brunswick County Court January 26th 1829
The above certificate was compared with the person of the above named ISAAC and found to be correct.

Teste R Turnbull CC

=====

Brunswick County to wit

I do hereby certify that the bearer hereof VIOLET GRAIN a free woman of light complexion five feet one and 5/8 inches high no visable scar aged about twenty five years, born free as appears by the evidence of W. ALLEN. Given under my hand this 25th day of August 1828.
(Entered before see register No. 279) R Turnbull CC

=====

Brunswick County to wit

I do hereby certify that the bearer hereof BILLY GRAIN a free man of year (sic) complexion five feet seven and a half Inches high about thirty years of age has a small scar in his forhead occasioned by a cut and one in the Bottom of the left foot from a cut also and no other scar visable was born free as appears from the evidence of JOHN WYCHE and by occupation a Sawyer. Given under my hand this 24th day of November 1828

Register No. 292 R Turnbull CC
W F Green JP (sic)

Brunswick County Court August Term 1828
The above certificate was compared with the person of the above named BILLY GRAIN and found to be correct

Teste R Turnbull CC

=====

Brunswick County to wit

I do hereby certify that the bearer hereof JEROME JAMES a free man of yellow complexion, five feet nine inches high about twenty one years old, has a scar on the right knee, with no other scar viserable scar and was born free as appears by the evidence of RANDOLPH PRICE. Given under my hand this 23rd day of February, One thousand Eight hundred and twenty nine

Register No 293 R Turnbull CC
John Wyche JP

Brunswick County Court February 23rd 1829

The above certificate was comapred with the person of the above named JEROME JAMES and found to be correct.

Teste R Turnbull CC

=====

Brunswick County to wit

I do hereby certify that the bearer hereof SUSAN WOODLEY a free woman of light complexion five feet five inches high with a scar on the left jaw aged nineteen years was born free as appears by the evidence of GEORGE C. DROMGOOLE & is duly registered in my office this 27th day of August 1827

Register No. 294 R Turnbull CC
Js. Rice JP

Brunswick County Court August Term 1827

The above certificate was compared with the person of the above named SUSAN WOODLEY and found to be correct.

Teste R Turnbull CC

=====

Brunswick County to wit

I do hereby certify that the bearer hereof JESSE CAIN a free man of colour about about (sic) twenty one years of age, five feet seven and a half inches high, has a scar in his forhead, one on his chin, several small ones on the back of his left hand, the fore finger of the right hand crooked, occasioned by the bite of a snake, with no other visable scars and was born free as appears by the evidence of JOHN WYCHE. Given under my hand this 25th day of August 1829

Register No. 295 R Turnbull CC
Js. Rice JP

Brunswick County Court August 25th 1829

The above certificate was compared with the person of the above named JESSE CAIN and found to be correct.

Teste R Turnbull CC

=====

Brunswick County to wit

I do hereby certify that the bearer hereof FANNY WOODLIEF a free woman of dark complexion five feet one inch and a half high, has no visable scar either on the head, face or arms, about forty four years old was emancipated by deed from EDWARD DROMGOOLE Sen. and is duly registered in my office this 28th day of September 1829

Register No. 296 R Turnbull CC
F. W. Green JP

Brunswick County Court September 28th 1829

The above certificate was compared with the person of the above named FANNY WOODLIEF and found to be correct.

Teste R Turnbull CC

=====

Brunswick County to wit

I do hereby certify that FANNY COLEMAN the bearer a free woman of light complexion five feet four inches high about twenty two years of age has no visable scar either on the hands, head or face and is one of the children of CATY who recovered her freedom from JOHN WYCHE in the Superior Court of Law of this County at the September Term of said Court 1819. Given under my hand this 28th day of September 1829

Register No. 297 R Turnbull CC
F W Green

Brunswick County Court September 28th 1829

The above certificate was compared with the person of the above named FANNY COLEMAN and found to be correct

Teste R Turnbull CC

=====

Brunswick County to wit

I do hereby certify that WM D KENNEDY a free man of dark complexion five feet eight inches high, about twenty nine years old, has one scar about two inches long on the right side of his neck and another shorter one immediately thereunder, the said WM D KENNEDY has no other visable scar either on his hands face or arms, and was born free as appears by an order of the Hustings Court of Richmond. Given under my hand this this (sic) 23rd day of Novem. 1829

Register No. 298 R Turnbull CC
Js. Rice JP

Brunswick County Court November 23rd 1829

The above certificate was compared with the person of the above named WM D KENNEDY and found to be correct

Teste R Turnbull CC

=====

Brunswick County to wit
I do hereby certify that GEORGE JONES the bearer hereof a free man of dark complexion, is five feet four inches and a half high, has no visable scar or mark either on his hands face or head, is about twenty two years of age, and was born free as appears by the evidence of JESSE KENNEDY. Given under my hand this 25th day of November 1829.

Regsiter No. 299 R Turnbull CC
John Wyche JP
Brunswick County Court November 25th 1829
The above certificate was compared with the person of the above named GEORGE JONES and found to be correct.
Teste R Turnbull

=====

Brunswick County to wit
I do Certify that ROBERT CROOK a free man of colour yellow complexion six feet high has a scar on the left side of his face extending from the forehead to the Cheek was born free as appears from a former Certificate which he has lost as appears by sufficient evidence about forty four years of age and is duly registered in my Office. Given under my hand this 28th day of December 1829.

Register No. 300 R Turnbull CC
Nathl E Mabry
Brunswick County Court December 28th 1829
The above Certificate was compared with the person of the above named ROBERT CROOK & found to be correct.

=====

Brunswick County to wit
I do hereby certify that the bearer hereof GREEN OWEN a free man of light complexion, about twenty three years of age, five feet, nine inches high, has a scar on the big toe of his right foot and another on the out side of his left leg, with none other perceivable, and was born free as appears by the evidence of NATHANIEL MITCHELL. Given under my hand this the 23rd day of February one thousand eight hundred and twenty nine

Register No. 301 R Turnbull CC
R F Pritchett
Brunswick County Court February 23rd 1829
The above certificate was compared with the person of the above named GREEN OWEN & found to be correct
Teste R Turnbull CC

=====

Brunswick County to wit

I hereby certify that the bearer hereof DANIEL JONES a free man of colour, about fifty seven years old, of yellow complexion five feet seven inches high, has a small scar below the left eye with no other mark or scar perceivable on his head, hands, face or arms. Is one of the slaves emancipated by EDW'D. DROMGOOLE by Deed of emancipation recorded in the County Court of Brunswick. Given under my hand this 22nd day of March 1830.

Register No. 302 R Turnbull CC

Brunswick County Court March 22nd 1830

The above certificate was compared with the person of the above named DANIEL JAMES and found to be correct.

Teste R Turnbull CC

=====

Brunswick County to wit

I do hereby certify that the bearer hereof CLAIBORNE EASTER a free man of colour five feet 11 inches high twenty one years of age has no scars or marks perceivable was born free as appears from the evidence of R H H WALTON and is duly registered in my office. Given under my hand this 26th day of July 1830

Register No. 303 R Turnbull CC

Brunswick County Court July 26th 1830

The above certificate was compared with the person of the said CLAIBORNE & found to be correct.

Teste R Turnbull CC

=====

Brunswick County to wit

I do certify that the bearer hereof HICKS GRAIN a free man of colour dark complexion 5 feet 5 Inches high about twenty two years of age has no scars or mark perceivable was born free as appears from the evidence of R H H WALLTON and is duly registered in my office. Given under my hand this 26th day of July 1830.

Register No. 304 R Turnbull CC

Brunswick County Court July 26th 1830

The above certificate was compared with the person of the said HICKS GRAIN & found to be correct.

Teste R Turnbull CC

=====

Brunswick County to wit

I do certify that the bearer hereof BILLY ROBERTS a free man of colour five feet five Inches high twenty one years of age one small scar over the right eye and no other mark perceivable was born free as appears by the evidence of BENJA. D CHAPMAN and is duly re-registered in my office. Given under my hand this 28th day of June 1830.

Register No. 305 R Turnbull CC
Edw'd. C Smith

Brunswick County Court June 28th 1830

The above certificate was compared with the person of the said BILLY ROBERTS & found to be correct.

Teste R Turnbull CC

=====

Brunswick County to wit

I do certify that the bearer hereof WYATT STEWART a free man of colour dark complexion five feet nine & a half Inches high about twenty three years of age has a scar on his right eye brow occasioned by a cut was born free as appears from the evidence of AUGUSTIN CLAIBORNE and is duly registered in my office. Given under my hand this 23rd day of August 1830

Register No. 306 R Turnbull CC
John Wyche

Brunswick County Court August 23rd 1830

The above certificate was compared with the person of the said WYATT STEWART & found to be Correct.

Teste R Turnbull CC

=====

Brunswick County to wit

I do certify that the bearer hereof BILLY GRAIN a free man of colour dark complexion five feet one & a half inches high about twenty three years of age has a scar over his right eye was born free as appears from the evidence of RICH'D. H. WALLTON and is duly registered in my office. Given under my hand this 26th day of July 1830.

Register No. 307 R Turnbull CC

E. C. Smith JP

Brunswick County Court July 26th 1830

The above certificate was compared with the person of the said BILLY GRAIN and found to be Correct.

Teste R Turnbull CC

=====

Brunswick County to wit

I do certify that the bearer hereof WILLIAM THOMPSON a free man of Colour about fifty three years of age, five feet seven inches high, has no scars perceivable, was born free as appears from the evidence of ROBERT HICKS and is duly registered in my office. Given under my hand this 25th day of October 1830

Register No. 308 R Turnbull CC
J. B. Mallory JP

Brunswick County Court October 25th 1830

The above certificate was compared with the person of the said WILLIA THOMPSON and found to be correct

Teste R Turnbull CC

=====

Brunswick County to wit

I do certify that the bearer hereof ITAY THOMAS a free woman of light complexion, about thirty two years of age, five feet one inch and a quarter in height, with two scars on the right arm, was born free as appears by the evidence of JOHN WYCHE, and is duly registered in my Office this 25th day of March 1828.

Register No. 309 R Turnbull CC
John Wyche JP

Brunswick County Court November 25th 1829

The above certificate was compared with the person of the said ITAY THOMAS and was found to be correct.

Teste R Turnbull CBC

=====

Brunswick County to wit

I do certify that the bearer hereof NED GRAIN a free man o Colour about thirty years of age, 5 feet six and a half inches high has a scar under the left side of the jaw another under the right ea and two others on the neck was born free as appears from the evidenc of JOHN WYCHE and is duly registered in my Office. Given under my hand this 25th day of July 1831.

Register No. 310 R Turnbull CC
E. C. Smith JP

Brunswick County Court July 25th 1831

The above certificate was Compared with the person of the said NED GRAIN and found to be correct.

Teste R Turnbull CBC

=====

Brunswick County to wit

I do certify that the bearer hereof NAT BUTCHER a free man of light complexion about forty four years old has a small scar on the left hand occasioned by a burn, and no other visable scar or mark either on the hands head or face, recovered his freedom from the executors of WILLIAM RICE dec'd in the Superior Court of Law of this County at the Septem. Term of said Court 1830. Given under my hand this 26th day of Septem. 1831.

Register No. 311 R Turnbull CBC
E. C. Smith JP

Brunswick County Court Septem. 26th 1831
The above certificate was compared with the person of the said NAT BUTCHER and found to be correct.

Teste R Turnbull CBC

=====

Brunswick County to wit

I do certify that the bearer hereof VINEY SEWARD a free woman of yellow complexion about thirty five years of age four feet ten inches high has a scar on the nail of the fourth finger of the left hand occasioned by a cut who it appears was emancipated by JOHN SEWARD of this County and is duly registered in my office. Given under my hand this 24th day of October 1831.

Register No. 312 R Turnbull CBC
F W Green JP

Brunswick County Court October 24th 1831
The above certificate was compared with the person of the above VINEY SEWARD and found to be correct.

Teste R Turnbull CC

=====

Brunswick County to wit

I do certify that the bearer hereof MACLIN SEWARD a free man of Colour five feet six and a half inches high about thirty years old has a scar on the right wrist occasioned by a burn was born free as appears by the evidence of JAMES J HARRISON and is duly Registered in my office. Given under my hand this 24th day of October 1831.

Registered No. 313 R Turnbull CBC
Benja. D Chapman JP

Brunswick County Court October 24th 1831
The above Certificate was compared with the person of the above MACLIN SEWARD and found to be correct.

Teste R Turnbull CBC

=====

Brunswick County to wit

I do certify that the bearer hereof RANDALL a free man of dark complexion about forty one years of age five feet five and a half inches high no scar or mark perceivable either on the hands head or face, is one of the children of AMY, (a free woman who was emancipated by JOHN SEWARD of this County) as appears by the evidence of a former certificate and is duly Registered in my office. Given under my hand this 24th day of October 1831.

Register No. 314 R Turnbull CBC
Benja. D Chapman JP

Brunswick County Court October 24th 1831

The above certificate was compared with the person of the above RANDALL & found to be correct.

Teste R Turnbull CC

=====

Brunswick County to wit

I do certify that the bearer hereof BETSEY MAYHO a free woman of colour about twenty four years of age five feet seven and a half inches high has a scar on the right Jaw was born free as appears by the evidence of DIGGS POYNOR and is duly Registered in my office this 24th day of October 1831.

Register No. 315 R Turnbull CBC
Benja. D Chapman JP

Brunswick County Court October 24th 1831

The above Certificate was compared with the person of the above BETSEY MAYHO and was found to be correct.

Teste R Turnbull CBC

=====

Brunswick County to wit

I do certify that the bearer hereof WILL COLEMAN a free man of dark complexion five feet six inches and a half high about fifty one years of age, has no scar or mark perceivable, either on the hands head or face recovered his freedom from the Admr. of WILLIAM W. HARPER dec'd in the Superior Court of Law of this County at the April Term of said Court 1818 and is duly registered in my office this 24th day of October 1831.

Register No. 316 R Turnbull CBC
Jno. Wyche JP

Brunswick County Court October 24th 1831

The above certificate was compared with the person of the above WILL COLEMAN & found to be correct.

Teste R Turnbull CC

=====

Brunswick County Court
I do certify that the bearer hereof PETER MAYS a free man of bright complexion about twenty two years of age five feet eight inches high has a small scar under the left eye one under the chin and several small ones on each hand and no others perceivable was born free as appears from the evidence of DIGGS POYNOR and is duly Registered in my Office. Given under my hand this 6th day of Septem. 1831.

Register No. 317 R Turnbull CBC
Benja. D Chapman JP
Brunswick County Court October 24th 1831
The foregoing certificate was compared with the person of the said PETER MAYS and found to be correct.
Teste R Turnbull CBC

=====

Brunswick County to wit
I do certify that the bearer hereof LEWIS MALONE a free man of dark complexion about twenty two years of age five feet nine inches high has no scar perceivable was born free as appears by the evidence of RICHARD W. FIELD and is duly Registered in my office. Given under my hand his 26th day of Septem. 1831

Register No. 318 R Turnbull CBC
Benja. D Chapman JP
Brunswick County Court October 24th 1831
The above certificate was compared with the person of the above LEWIS MALONE and found to be correct.
Teste R Turnbull CBC

=====

Brunswick County to wit
I do certify that the bearer hereof NAPOLEON PRICE a free man of light complexion about twenty one years old five feet four inches and a quarter high has a small scar over the left eye and no ther mark perceivable was born free as appears by the evidence of BENJAMIN D CHAPMAN and is duly Registered in my office this 26th day of Septem. 1831.

Register No. 319
Isham Trotter JP
Brunswick County Court October 24th 1831
The above Certificate was compared with the person of the above NAPOLEON PRICE and found to be correct.
Teste R Turnbull CBC

=====

Brunswick County to wit

I do certify that the bearer hereof JOHN JONES a free man of colour about twenty two years of age, five feet, five, inches high and has no scars perceivable was born free as appears from the evidence of NEHEMIAH NOLLEY and is duly Registered in my Office. Given under my hand this 27th day of Septem. 1830.

Register No. 320
John Manning

Brunswick County Court October 24th 1831

The above Certificate was compared with the person ofthe above JOHN JONES and found to be correct.

Teste R Turnbull CBC

=====

Brunswick County to wit

I do Certify that the bearer hereof NAT MOSS a free man of dark complexion about forty one years old five feet nine inches high has a scar on the inside of the right arm just below the elbow and another on the back of his left hand was born free as appears by TILLMAN AVERY and is duly Registered in my office. Given under my hand this 24th day of October 1831.

Register No. 321 R Turnbull CBC
Jno. Manning

Brunswick County Court October 24th 1831

The above certificate was compared with the person of the above NAT MOSS and found to be correct.

Teste R Turnbull CBC

=====

Brunswick County to wit

I do certify that the bearer hereof CRESY POMPEY a free woman of dark complexion about thirty six years old five feet two inches high has no scar or mark perceivable either on the hands head or face as appears from the evidence of PHEBE HARRISON and is duly Registered in my office this 26th day of Septem. 1831.

Register No. 322 R Turnbull CBC
John Wych JP

Brunswick County Court October 24th 1831

The above certificate was compared with the person of the above CRESY POMPEY and found to be correct.

Teste R Turnbull CBC

=====

Brunswick County to wit

I do certify that the bearer hereof DAVID MERRITT a free man of dark complexion about thirty five years old five feet eight inches and a half high has a small scar on the right side of the face another on the left hand and no others perceivable was born free as appears by the evidence of a former certificate and is duly Registered in my Office. Given under my hand this 26th day of Septem. 1831.

Register No. 323 R Turnbull CBC

F. W. Green JP

Brunswick County Court October 24th 1831

The above certificate was compared with the person of the said DAVID MERRITT and found to be correct.

Teste R Turnbull CBC

=====

Brunswick County to wit

I do certify that the bearer hereof PASCAL MERRITT a free man of dark complexion about twenty six years old five feet ten inches and a half high has a long scar on the right wrist and no other scar or mark perceivable either on the hands head or face was born free as appears by the evidence of EDWARD C. SMITH and JOS. J. G. TUCKER and is duly Registered in my Office. Given under my hand this 26th day of Septem. 1831.

Register No. 324 R Turnbull CBC

F W Green JP

Brunswick County Court October 24th 1831

The above certificate was compared with the person of the said PASCAL MERRITT and found to be correct.

Teste R Turnbull CBC

=====

Brunswick County to wit

I do certify that the bearer hereof BETSEY POMPEY a free woman of dark complexion about sixty years old five feet four inches high has a small scar above the left eye and another in the forehead and no others perceivable was born free as appears by the evidence of PHEBE HARRISON and is duly Registered in my Office this 26th day of September 1831.

Register No. 325 R Turnbull CBC

John Wyche JP

Brunswick County Court October 24th 1831

The above certificate was compared with the person of the said BETSEY POMPEY and found to be correct.

Teste R Turnbull CBC

=====

Brunswick County to wit

I do certify that the bearer hereof MARY ANN WALKER a free woman of Dark complexion about twenty eight years of age, five feet three inches and a half high has a scar on on (sic) her wrist, was born free as appears by the evidence of WILLIAM SAMFORD and is duly Registered in my Office this 28th day of November 1831.

Register No. 326 R Turnbull CBC
A. Powell JP

Brunswick County Court November 28th 1831

The above certificate was compared with the person of the said MARY ANN WALKER and found to be correct.

Teste R Turnbull CBC

=====

Brunswick County to wit

I do certify that the bearer hereof MONROE PRICE a free man of light complexion about twenty one years of age, five feet, five and half inches high, has a small scar over the left eye and no other mark or scar perceivable either on the hands head or face was born free as appears by the evidence of JOHN S. HARRIS and is duly Registered in my Office this 25th day of Ocotber AD 1831.

Register No. 327 R Turnbull CBC
John Wyche

Brunswick County Court November Term 1831

The above certificate was compared with the person of the said MONROE PRICE and found to be correct.

Teste R Turnbull CC

=====

Brunswick County to wit

I do certify that the bearer hereof JACOB MERRITT a free man of dark complexion about thirty seven years of age five feet f[illegible] inches high has a small scar on the left jaw another on the middle f[illegible]ger of the left hand and no others perceivable, was born free as app[illegible] from a former certificate and is duly Registered in Office. Given under my hand this 26th day of Decem. 1831.

Register No. 328
Jno. Wyche JP

Brunswick County Court Dec. 26th 1831

The above certificate was compared with the person of the said JACOB MERRITT and found to be correct.

Teste R Turnbull CC

=====

Brunswick County to wit

I do certify that the bearer hereof HENRY WALKER a free man of light complexion about twenty five years of age five feet, eleven and a half inches high, has a scar on the lower part of the left thumb and no other scar or mark perceivable was born free as appears by the evidence of WILLIAM SAMFORD and is duly Registered in my Office this 28th day of Novem. 1831.

Register No. 329 R Turnbull CBC
A. Powell JP

Brunswick County Court Novem. 28th 1831
The above certificate was compared with the person of the said HENRY WALKER and found to be correct.

Teste R Turnbull CBC

=====

Brunswick County to wit

I do certify that the bearer hereof MOSES WALKER a free man of dark complexion about twenty one years of age, five feet, eight inches high has no scar or mark perceivable either on the hands head or face was born free as appears by the evidence of WILLIAM SAMFORD and is duly Registered in my Office this 28th day of November AD 1831.

Register No. 330 R Turnbull CBC
A Powell JP

Brunswick County Court Novem. 28th 1831
The above certificate was compared with the person of the said MOSES WALKER and found to be correct.

Teste R Turnbull CBC

=====

Brunswick County to wit

I do certify that the bearer hereof KIZZY CROOK a free woman of light complexion about fifty four years of age five feet five inches high has no scar or mark perceivable either on the hands or face was born free as appears by the evidence of ROBERT TURNBULL and is duly Registered in my Office this 3rd day of December 1831.

Register No. 331 R Turnbull CBC
Burwell B Wilkes JP

Brunswick County Court Jany. 23rd 1832
The above certificate was compared with the person of the said KIZZY CROOK and found to be correct.

Teste R Turnbull CC

=====

Brunswick County to wit
I do certify that the bearer hereof AMOS a free man of yellow complexion about thirty four years of age five feet eleven inches high has a scar on the forefinger of the left hand and also a scar on each elbow and no other scar or mark perceivable either on the hands or face recovered his freedom from DAVID HOBBS in the Superior Court of Law of Brunswick County by occupation a blacksmith, and is duly Registered in my Office. Given under my hand this 29th day of Nov. 1831.

Register No. 332 R Turnbull CBC
A. Powell JP

Brunswick County Court November 29th 1831
The above certificate was compared with the person of the said AMOS and found to be correct.

Teste R Turnbull CBC

=====

Brunswick County to wit
I do certify that the bearer hereof LUCETTA MORSE a free woman of dark complexion about twenty four years old five feet four inches high has no visable scar or mark, either on the head hands or face, was born free as appears by the evidence of EDWARD C. SMITH and is duly Registered in my Office this 26th day of Septem. 1831.

Register No. 333 R Turnbull CBC

Brunswick County Court November Term 1831
The above certificate was compared with the person of the said LUCETTA MORSE and found to be correct.

Teste R Turnbull CC

=====

Brunswick County to wit
I do certify that the bearer hereof MORTON MERRITT a free man of dark complexion, about twenty three years of age, five feet ten inches high has a scar on the left jaw, another on the bottom lip, and each little finger bent, was born free as appears by the evidence of ________ and is duly Registered in my office. Given under my hand this 26th day of March 1832.

Register No. 334 R Turnbull CBC
John Tucker

Brunswick County Court March 26th 1832
The above certificate was compared with the person of the said MERRITT and found to be correct.

Teste R Turnbull CBC

=====

Brunswick County to wit

I do certify that the bearer hereof JOHN H. WALKER a free man of dark complexion about twenty one years of age five feet eight and a half inches high, has a small scar on the left jaw occasioned by a burn and no others perceivable, was born free as appears, and is duly Registered in my Office. Given under my hand this 27th day of March 1832.

Register No. 335 R Turnbull CC
John Wyche JP

Brunswick County Court April 23rd 1832

The above certificate was compared with the person of the said JOHN H. WALKER and found to be correct.

Teste R Turnbull CBC

=====

Brunswick County to wit

I do certify that the bearer hereof PRISSY EVANS a free woman of dark compelxion, about twenty one years of age five feet, 3 3/4 inches high has a small scar over the right eye, and no others perceivable, either on the hands, head or face, was born free and is duly Registered in my office, this 27 day of March 1832.

Register No. 336 R Turnbull CC
Creed Haskins JP

Brunswick County Court April Term 1832

The foregoing certificate was compared with the person of the said PRISSY EVANS and found to be correct.

Teste R Turnbull CC

=====

Brunswick County to wit

I do certify that EDMUND OWEN the bearer hereof a free man of light complexion about twenty one years of age, five feet, eight & ½ inches high has a scar on the back of the left hand, and no others perceivable, was born free as appears by the evidence of JAMES HARRISON, and is duly Registered in my Office this 23rd day of July 1832.

Register No. 337 R Turnbull CC
John Wyche JP

Brunswick County Court July 23rd 1832

The above certificate was compared with the person of the said EDMUND OWEN and found to be correct.

Teste R Turnbull CBC

=====

Brunswick County to wit

I do certify that the bearer hereof FEATHERSTON MERRITT a free man of dark complexion about twenty one years of age, five feet, five & ½ inches high, has no scar or mark perceivable, either on the hands head or face, was born free as appears by the evidence of F W GREEN, and is duly Registered in my Office.this 27th day of August 1832.

Register No. 338 R Turnbull CBC

John Wyche JP

Brunswick County Court August 27th 1832

The above certificate was compared with the person of the said FEATHERSTON MERRITT and found to be correct.

Teste R Turnbull CBC

=====

Brunswick County to wit

I do certify that the bearer hereof JACK ROBERTS a free man of dark complexion, five feet, eleven inches high, has a scar on the back of the right hand between the fingers, twenty four years of age, was born free as appears from the evidence of F. W. GREEN and is duly Registered in my Office this 27th day of August 1832.

Register No. 339 R Turnbull CBC

John Wyche JP

Brunswick County Court August 27th 1832

The above certificate was compared with the person of the said JACK ROBERTS and found to be correct.

Teste R Turnbull CBC

=====

Brunswick County to wit

I do certify that the bearer hereof ALLEN CAIN a free man of dark complexion about twenty eight years of age, five feet ten & 3/4 inches high, has a scar on the right arm and one on the left and no others perceivable, was born free as appears by a former certificate and is duly Registered in my Office. Given under my hand this 27th day of August 1832.

Register No. 340 R Turnbull CBC

F. W. Green JP

Brunswick County Court August 27th 1832

The above certificate was compared with the person of the said ALLEN CAIN and found to be correct.

Teste R Turnbull CBC

=====

Brunswick County to wit
I do certify that the bearer hereof THEODORICK WALKER a free man of light complexion about twenty five years of age, five feet ten & ½ inches high, has a small scar in the forehead, just above the left eye and no other scar or mark perceivable either on the hands head or face is one of the slaves emancipated by PETER ROBINSON Executor of BENJAMIN JONES dec'd who was Executor of WILLIAM WALKER dec'd by deed of emancipation Recorded in the County Court of Brunswick and is duly Registered in my Office this 27th day of August 1832.

Register No. 341 R Turnbull CBC
E. C. Smith JP

Brunswick County Court August 27th 1832
The above certificate was compared with the person of the said THEODORICK WALKER and found to be correct.

Teste R Turnbull CBC

=====

Brunswick County to wit
I do certify that the bearer hereof ROWANA POMPEY a free woman of dark complexion about twenty years old, five feet two inches high, has no visable scars either on the hands, head or face was born free as appears by the evidence of JOHN WYCHE, and is duly Registered in my Office this 26th day of September 1831.

Register No. 342 R Turnbull CBC
Creed Haskins JP

Brunswick County Court August Term 1832
The above certificate was compared with the person of the said ROWANA POMPEY and found to be correct.

Teste R Turnbull CBC

=====

Brunswick County to wit
I do certify that the bearer hereof GREEN COLEMAN a free man of dark complexion, about twenty one years old, five feet seven inches and a quarter high, has a small scar on the left wrist occasioned by a burn, and no other scar or mark perceivable, either on the hands head or face, and is one of the children of CATY who recovered her freedom from JOHN WYCHE in the Superior Court of Law of this County at this September Term of said Court 1819. Given under my hand this 26th day of September 1831.

Register No. 343 R Turnbull CBC
F. W. Green JP

Brunswick County Court August Term 1832
The above certificate was compared with the person of the said GREEN COLEMAN and found to be correct.

Teste R Turnbull CBC

=====

Brunswick County to wit

I do certify that the bearer hereof LUCINDA POMPEY a free woman of dark complexion about twenty years of age, five feet and a half inch high has two small scars on the back of the right hand, and no others perceivable, was born free as appears by the evidence of JOHN WYCHE and is duly Registered in my Office this 28th day of November 1831.

Register No. 344 R Turnbull CBC
E. C. Smith JP

Brunswick County Court August Term 1832
The above certificate was compared with the person of the said LUCINDA POMPEY and found to be correct.

Teste R Turnbull CBC

=====

Brunswick County to wit

I do certify that the bearer hereof WILLIAM ATKINS a free man of dark complexion about twenty one years of age, five feet ten & ½ inches high, has a scar on the back of the right hand and no oth perceivable, was born free as appears by the evidence of FREDERICK W. GREEN and is duly Registered in my Office this 27th day of Augus AD 1832.

Registered No. 345 R Turnbull CBC

E. C. Smith JP

Brunswick County Court August Term 1832
The above certificate was compared with the person of the said WILLI ATKINS and was found to be correct.

Teste R Turnbull CBC

=====

Brunswick County to wit

I do hereby certify that the bearer hereof MARTHA CAIN a free woman of yellow complexion five feet two inches high, nineteen years of age, looks a little cross eyed, has no scar or mark perceivable, was born free as appears from the evidence of FREDERICK W. GREEN and is duly Registered, in my Office this 27th day of August 1832.

Register No. 346 R Turnbull CBC
E C Smith JP

Brunswick County Court August Term 1832
The above certificate was compared with the person of the said MARTHA CAIN and found to be correct.

Teste R Turnbull CBC

=====

Brunswick County to wit
I do hereby certify that the bearer hereof BETSY CAIN a free woman of brown complexion five feet four inches high, about thirty five years of age, has a scar on the back of the right hand, was born free as appears from the evidence of F. W. GREEN and is duly Registered in my Office this 27th day of August 1832.

Register No. 347 R Turnbull CBC
E. C. Smith JP
Brunswick County Court August Term
The above certificate was compared with the person of the said BETSY CAIN and found to be correct.
Teste R Turnbull CBC

=====

Brunswick County to wit
I do hereby certify that NANCY EASTER the bearer hereof a free woman of black complexion, thirty years old five feet six inches high, has a scar on the head above the left temple, was born free as appears from the evidence of F. W. GREEN, and is duly Registered in my Office this 27th day of August 1832.

Register No. 348 R Turnbull CC
Creed Haskins JP
Brunswick County Court August Term 1832
The above certificate was compared with the person of the said NANCY EASTER and found to be correct.
Teste R Turnbull CBC

=====

Brunswick County to wit
I do hereby certify that the bearer hereof MIMY CAIN a free woman of dark complexion, about twenty five years old, five feet, five inches high, has no scar or mark perceivable, either on the hands head or face, was born free as appears by the evidence of JOHN WYCHE, and is duly Registered in my Office this 27th day of August AD 1832.

Register No. 349 R Turnbull CBC
F. W. Green JP
Brunswick County Court August Term 1832
The above certificate was compared with the person of the said MIMY CAIN and found to be correct.
Teste R Turnbull CBC

=====

Brunswick County to wit
I do certify that the bearer hereof LUCY GRAIN a free woman of dark complexion about nineteen years of age, five feet one & ¼ inches high, has a scar behind the left ear, and no others perceivable, either on the hands head or face, was born free as appears by the evidence of F. W. GREEN and is duly Registered in my Office this 27th day of August 1832.

Register No. 350 R Turnbull CBC
E. C. Smith JP
Brunswick County Court August Term 1832
The above certificate was compared with the person of the said LUCY GRAIN and found to be correct.
Teste R Turnbull CBC

=====

Brunswick County to wit
I do certify that the bearer hereof ANN EASTER a free woman of dark complexion about twenty four years of age, five feet, nine & ¼ inches high, has several small scars on the back of each hand, and no others perceivable, was born free as appears by the evidence of F. W. GREEN, and is duly Registered in my Office this 27th day of August 1832.

Register No. 351 R Turnbull CBC
Creed Haskins JP
Brunswick County Court August Term 1832
The above certificate was compared with the person of the said ANN EASTER and found to be correct.
Teste R Turnbull CBC

=====

Brunswick County to wit
I do certify that the bearer hereof MURFREE B.T. STEWART a free man of yellow complexion about twenty six years of age, six feet one inch and a half high, has a small scar near the right eye, occasioned by a burn, one in the palm of his left hand, and one of the fingers of his right hand swelled at the end, occasioned by its having been broken, and no others perceivable, was born free as appears by the evidence of JOHN WYCHE, and is duly Registered in my Office this 7th day of September AD 1832.

Register No. 352 R Turnbull CBC
Robert Jackson JP
Brunswick County Court September Term 1832
The above certificate was compared with the person of the said STEWART and found to be correct.
Teste R Turnbull CBC

=====

Brunswick County to wit

I do certify that the bearer hereof PARKER POMPEY a free man of dark complexion, about twenty five years of age, five feet seven inches high, has a small scar on the left wrist, and no others perceivable, was born free as appears by the evidence of JOHN WYCHE and is duly Registered in my Office this 22nd day of October 1832.

Register No. 353 R Turnbull CBC
B B Wilkes JP

Brunswick County Court October Term 1832

The foregoing certificate was compared with the person of the said PARKER POMPEY and found to be correct.

Teste R Turnbull CBC

=====

Brunswick County to wit

I do certify that the bearer hereof GREEN OWEN a free man of light complexion, about twenty six years of age, five feet nine inches high, has no scar or mark perceivable either on the hands head or face, was born free as appears by a former certificate, and is duly Registered in my Office. Given under my hand this 26th day of November 1832.

Register No. 354 R Turnbull CBC
Burwell B. Wilkes

Brunswick County Court November 26th 1832

The above certificate was compared with the person of the said GREEN OWEN and found to be correct.

Teste R Turnbull CBC

=====

Brunswick County to wit

I do certify that the bearer hereof HENRY OWEN a free man of dark complexion, about twenty one years of age, five feet seven & ½ inches high, has a small scar on the left eye lid and no others perceivable, was born free as appears by the evidence of R. H. H. WALLTON and is duly Registered in my Office, this 28th day of January 1833.

Register No. 355 R Turnbull CBC
Wm Meredith

Brunswick County Court January 28th 1833

The above certificate was compared with the person of the said HENRY OWEN and found to be correct.

Teste R Turnbull

=====

Brunswick County to wit

I do certify that the bearer hereof POLLY GRAIN a free woman of dark complexion about twenty seven years of age, five feet two & ¼ inches high, has no scar or mark perceivable, either on the hands head or face, was born free as appears by the evidence of R. H. H. WALLTON, and is duly Registered in my Office this 25th day of March 1833.

Registered No. 356 R Turnbull CBC
John Wyche JP

Brunswick County Court March 25th 1833

The above certificate was compared with the person of said POLLY GRAIN and found to be correct.

Teste R Turnbull

=====

Brunswick County to wit

I do certify that the bearer hereof MATTHEW GRAIN a free man of dark complexion, about twenty seven years of age, five feet seven inches high, has several small scars on the back of the left hand and no others perceivable, was born free as appears by a former certificate, and is duly Registered in my Office this 27th day of May 183

Registered No. 357 R Turnbull CBC
John Wyche

Brunswick County Court April 27th 1833

The above certificate was compared with the person of the said MATTHEW GRAIN and found to be correct.

Teste R Turnbull CBC

=====

Brunswick County to wit

I do hereby certify that the bearer hereof DANIEL JAMES a free man of colour about sixty years of age of yellow complexion five feet six and one half inches high has a small scar below the left eye and no other scar or mark perceivable either on the hands head or face, is one of the slaves emancipated by EDWARD DROMGOOLE by Deed of emancipation recorded in the County Court and is duly Registered in my Office, Given under my hand this 8th day of May 1833.

Register No. 358 R Turnbull CBC
F. W. Green JP

Brunswick County Court April 27th 1833

The above certificate was compared with the person of the said DANIEL JAMES and found to be correct.

Teste R Turnbull CBC

=====

Brunswick County to wit
I do certify that the bearer hereof ALFRED CAIN a free man of dark complexion about twenty two years of age, five feet, seven and a half inches high, has several scars on the back of each hand occasioned by burns, one over his left eye and no others perceivable, was born free as appears by the evidence of THOMAS S. GHOLSON, and is duly Registered in my Office this 12th day of March 1832.

Register No. 359 R Turnbull CBC
Burwell B. Wilkes JP
Brunswick County Court August Term 1833
The above certificate was compared with the person of the said ALFRED CAIN & found to be correct.
Teste R Turnbull CBC

=====

Brunswick County to wit
I do certify that the bearer hereof HARRIET MERRITT a free woman of dark complexion about twenty four years of age five feet and one half inch high has no scar or mark perceivable either on the hands head or face, is one of the Children of CATY MERRITT who was emancipated by HENRY MERRITT of this County by Deed of emancipation Recorded in Brunswick County Court and is duly Registered in my Office this 23rd day of Septem. 1833.

Register No. 360 R Turnbull CBC
W. Palmer JP
Brunswick County Court Sep. 23rd 1833
The above certificate was compared with the person of the said HARRIET MERRITT and found to be correct.
Teste R Turnbull CBC

=====

Brunswick County to wit
I do certify that the bearer hereof WILSON EVANS a free man of colour about twenty one years of age, five feet nine inches high, has no scar or mark perceivable either on the hands head or face, is one of the children of CHARLOTTE EVANS who was emancipated by OWEN MYRICK of this County, as appears from the evidence of B. D. CHAPMAN and is duly Registered in my Office this 22nd day of July AD 1833.

Register No. 361 R Turnbull CBC

W. Palmer JP
Brunswick County Court Sep. 23rd 1833
The above certificate was compared with the person of the sd WILSON EVANS & found to be correct.
Teste R Turnbull CBC

=====

Brunswick County to wit

I do certify that the bearer hereof BERRY CAIN a free man of dark complexion about twenty six years of age five feet eleven en and one half inches high has no scar or mark perceivable either on th hands head or face, was born free as appears from the evidence of ___ ________ and is duly Registered in my Office this 23rd day of September 1833.

Register No. 362 R Turnbull CBC
Benja. D. Chapman JP

Brunswick County Court September 23rd 1833
The above certificate was compared with the person of the said BERRY CAIN and found to be correct.

Teste R Turnbull CBC

=====

Brunswick County to wit

I do certify that the bearer hereof ABRAHAM ROBERTS a free man of dark complexion about twenty eight years of age five feet eigh inches high, has a Scar on the left thumb and no others perceivable, was born free as appears from the evidence of ______________ and is duly Registered in my Office this 23rd day of Septem. 1833

Registered No. 363 R Turnbull CBC
Jno. Manning JP

Brunswick County Court September 23rd 1833
The above certificate was compared with the person of the said ABRAHAM ROBERTS and found to be correct.

Teste R Turnbull CBC

=====

Brunswick County to wit

This is to certify that the bearer hereof BOB JAMES a free man of color about sixty six years of age five feet seven Inches hig has no scar perceivable is dim sighted in the right eye, and was eman cipated by OWEN MYRICK as appears from a former certificate & is dul registered in my Office. Given under my hand this 27th day of Janua 1834.

Register No. 364 R Turnbull CBC
F. W. Green JP

Brunswick County Court January 27th 1834
The above certificate was compared with the person of the above BOB JAMES & found to be correct.

Teste R Turnbull CBC

=====

Brunswick County to wit

I do certify that the bearer hereof CHARLOTTE EVANS a free woman of color about forty five years of age five feet & half an Inch high has no scar or mark perceivable either on the hand head or face is one of the slaves emancipated by OWEN MYRICK of this County & is duly registered in my office this 22nd day of July AD 1833.

Register No. 365
F. W. Green JP

Brunswick County Court January 27th 1834

The above certificate was compared with the person of the above CHARLOTTE EVANS & found to be correct.

Teste R Turnbull CC

=====

Brunswick County to wit

This is to certify that the bearer hereof WM. PRICE a free man of Color about twenty one years of age five feet six Inches high has no scar or mark perceivable was born free as appears from the evidence of F. W. GREEN and is duly registered in my office. Given under my hand this 27th day of January 1834.

Registered No. 366 R Turnbull CC
John Wyche JP

Brunswick County Court January 27th 1834

The above certificate was compared with the person of the above WM. PRICE & found to be correct.

Teste R Turnbull CC

=====

Brunswick County to wit

I do hereby certify that the bearer hereof CLARISSA EASTER a free woman of color dark complexion five feet four Inches high fifty years of age has no scar or mark perceivable except one on the forehead, was emancipated by OWEN MYRICK as appears by a deed of emancipation. Given under my hand this 25th day of March 1834.

Register No. 367 R Turnbull CC
John Wyche JP

Brunswick County Court March 25th 1834

The above certificate was compared with the person of the above CLARISSA & found to be correct.

Teste R Turnbull CC

=====

Brunswick County to wit

I do hereby certify that the bearer hereof BILLY CAIN a free man of color five feet eight Inches high about twenty two years old was born free as appears from the eivdence of R H H WALLTON & is duly registered in my office. Given under my hand this 25th day of August 1834.

Register No. 368 R Turnbull CC
Benja. D Chapman JP

Brunswick County Court August 25th 1834.

The within Certificate was compared with the person of the above BILLY CAIN & found to be correct.

Teste R Turnbull CC

=====

Brunswick County to wit,

I do hereby certify that the bearer hereof ALLEN MOORE a free man of color five feet seven inches high, forty eight years old, one or two small scars on the left hand and was born free as appears from the evidence of WM H ELDRIDGE and is duly registered in my Office. Given under my hand this 25th day of August 1834.

Register No. 369 R Turnbull CC
Benja D Chapman JP

Brunswick County Court August 25th 1834

The within Certificate was compared with the person of the above ALLEN MOORE & found to be correct.

Teste R Turnbull CC

=====

Brunswick County to wit

I do hereby certify that the bearer hereof JOANNA DANIEL a free woman of color yellow complexion five feet one Inch high about twenty five years old has a scar on the back of the right hand occasioned by a burn was born free as appears by the evidence of BENJA. D CHAPMAN and is duly registered in my Office. Given under my hand this 27th day of October 1834.

Register No. 370 R Turnbull CC
Benja. D. Chapman JP

Brunswick County Court October 27th 1834

The above certificate was compared with the person of the above JOANNA DANIEL & found to be correct.

Teste R Turnbull CC

=====

Brunswick County to wit
I do hereby certify that the bearer hereof NANCY ROBERTS a free woman of color dark complexion five feet four Inches high about twenty three years old has a small scar on the left hand was born free as appears by the evidence of BENJA. D, CHAPMAN & is duly registered in my office. Given under my hand this 27 day of October 1834.

Register No. 371 R Turnbull CC
Benja. D. Chapman
Brunswick County Court October 27th 1834
The above certificate was compared with the person of the above NANCY ROBERTS & found to be correct.
Teste R Turnbull CC

=====

Brunswick County to wit
I do hereby certify that the bearer hereof PEGGY HENDERSON a free woman of color dark complexion five feet high about twenty two years old has a scar on the right hand & one on the neck was born free as appears from the evidence of RICHARD F. PRITCHETT and is duly registered in my office. Given under my hand this 24th day of November 1834.

Register No. 372 R Turnbull CC
John Tucker
Brunswick County Court November 24th 1834
The above certificate was compared with the person of the above PEGGY HENDERSON & found to be correct.
Teste R Turnbull CC

=====

Brunswick County to wit
I do hereby certify that the bearer hereof JAMES CAIN a free man of color five feet seven inches high about forty three years old the forefinger on the right hand being cut off was emancipated by OWEN MYRICK as appears from a former certificate and is duly registered in my office. Given under my hand this 25th day of August 1834.

Register No. 373 R Turnbull CC
Benja. D. Chapman JP
Brunswick County Court August Term 1835
The above certificate was compared with the person of the said JAMES CAIN & found to be correct.
Teste R Turnbull CC

=====

Brunswick County to wit

I do hereby certify that the bearer hereof POLLY CAIN a free woman of color five feet two Inches high about twenty five years old was born free as appears from the evidence of R H H WALLTON and is duly registered in my office. Given under my hand this 25th day of August 1834

Register No. 374 R Turnbull CC
Benja. D. Chapman JP

Brunswick County Court August Term 1834

The above certificate was compared with the person of the above POLLY CAIN & found to be correct.

Teste R Turnbull CC

=====

Brunswick County to wit

I do hereby certify that the bearer hereof DEMSEY EASTER a free man of Colour five feet nine Inches high twenty one years old has a scar on the left side of the chin was born free as appears from the evidence of R. H. H. WALLTON and is duly registered in my Office. Given under my hand this 25th day of May 1835.

Register No. 375 R Turnbull CC
Burwell B Wilkes

Brunswick County Court May Term 1835

The above certificate was compared with the person of the said DEMPSEY EASTER and found to be correct.

Teste R Turnbull CC

=====

Brunswick County to wit

I do hereby certify that the bearer hereof ROBERT BUTLER a free man of color dark complexion about forty five years of age five feet eight Inches high one scar on the upper lip was born free as appears from the eivdence of WM. SCARBOROUGH and is duly registered in my office. Given under my hand this 25th day of May 1835.

Register No. 376 R Turnbull CC
Jos. A. Riddick JP

Brunswick County Court May Term 1835

The above certificate was compared with the person of the above ROBERT & found to be correct.

R Turnbull CC

=====

Brunswick County to wit
I do hereby certify that the bearer hereof SUSANNA BOWEN a free woman of color yellow complexion five feet one Inch high twenty four years old has a scar under the left cheek was born free as appears from the evidence of HARTWELL HILL and is duly registered in my office. Given under my hand this 24th day of December 1834.

Register No. 377
Wm. Meredith JP

Brunswick County Court December Term 1834
The above certificate was compared with the person of the above SUSANNA BOWEN & found to be correct.

Teste R Turnbull CBC

=====

Brunswick County to wit
I do certify that the bearer hereof ANNA OWEN a free woman of light complexion about 39 years of age 5 feet 3½ Inches high has a long scar in in (sic) the forehead and several small ones on the back of each hand and no others perceivable was born free as appears by the evidence of EDWARD C. SMITH and is duly registered in my office this 24th day of Sept. 1832.

Register No. 378 R Turnbull
Robert Jackson JP

Brunswick County Court September Term 1832
The above certificate was compared with the person of ANNA OWEN and found to be correct.

Teste R Turnbull CBC

=====

Brunswick County to wit
I do certify that the bearer hereof HANNAH ATKINS a free woman of dark complexion about twenty six years of age five feet six inches high has no scar or mark perceivable either on the hands head or face was born free as appears from the evidence of R. H. H. WALLTON and is duly Registered in my office. Given under my hand this 28th day of October 1833.

Register No. 379 R Turnbull CBC
Wm. Meredith JP

Brunswick County Court September Term 1835
The above Certificate was compared with the person of the said HANNAH ATKINS and found to be correct.

Teste R Turnbull CBC

=====

Brunswick County to wit

I do certify that the bearer hereof MIKE ATKINS a free man of dark complexion about thirty five years of age six feet high has no scar or mark perceivable either on the hands head or face was born free as appears from the evidence of BENJA. PHIPPS and is duly Registered in my office. Given under my hand this 23rd day of September 1833.

Register No. 380 R Turnbull CC
Wm. Meredith JP

Brunswick County Court September 28th 1835
The above Certificate was compared with the person of the above MIKE ATKINS and found to be correct.

Teste R Turnbull CBC

=====

Brunswick County to wit

I do certify that the bearer hereof DOLLY ATKINS a free woman of dark complexion about thirty five years of age four feet eleven inches high has no scar or mark perceivable either on the hands head or face was born free as appears from the evidence of BENJA. PHIPPS and is duly Registered in my office this 28th day of October 1833.

Register No. 381 R Turnbull CBC
Wm. Meredith JP

Brunswick County Court September 28th 1835.
The above Certificate was compared with the person of the above DOLLY ATKINS & found to be correct.

Teste R Turnbull CBC

=====

Brunswick County to wit

I do hereby Certify that HARRIAN EDMUNSON a free girl of yellow complexion five feet five inches high about 22 years of age was born free as appears from the evidence of N. T. EDMUNDS and is duly Registered in my office this 28th day of September 1835.

Register No. 382 R Turnbull CC
Wm. Meredith JP

Brunswick County Court Sept. 28th 1835
The above Certificate was compared with the person of the above HARRIANE EDMUNSON and found to be correct.

Teste R Turnbull CBC

=====

Brunswick County to wit

I do certify that the bearer hereof WINNY HERCULEUS a free woman bright mulatto five feet one inch high about forty five years of age has a scar under the corner of her right eye and a mole on the tip end of the nose has been duly Registered in the clerks office the County Court of Dinwiddie and was allowed to remain in this state by an order of the said County Court of Dinwiddie as appears by a Copy of the said order and is duly registered in my office this 28th day of Sept 1835.

Register No. 383 R Turnbull CC

Brunswick County Court Sept 28th 1833

The above Certificate was compared with the person of the above WINNY HERCULEUS and found to be correct.

Teste R Turnbull CBC

=====

Brunswick County to wit

I do hereby certify that the bearer hereof PASCAL EASTER a free man of colour five feet seven inches high Twenty two years old has no scar or mark perceivable was born free as appears from the evidence of RICHARD H. H. WALLTON and is duly Registered in my office. Given under my hand this 28th day of September 1835.

Register No. 384 R Turnbull CC

Wm. Meredith JP

Brunswick County Court Sept 28th 1835

The above Certificate was compared with the person of the above PASCAL EASTER and found to be correct.

R Turnbull

=====

Brunswick County to wit

I do certify that the bearer hereof ELCE MALONE a free woman of dark complexion about twenty five years of age five feet two Inches high has no scar or mark perceivable either on the hands head or face was born free as appears from the evidence of JARROT ABERNATHY and is duly Registered in my office this 26th day of October 1835.

Register No. 385 R Turnbull CC

Wm. Meredith JP

Brunswick County Court October 26th 1835

The above Certificate was compared with the person of the above ELCE MALONE and found to be correct.

R Turnbull CC

=====

Brunswick County to wit

I do certify that the bearer hereof MARY MALONE a free woman of dark complexion about twenty three years of age five feet two inches high has no scar or mark perceivable either on the hands or face was born free as appears from the evidence of BUCKNER ABERNATHY and is duly Registered in my office this 26th day of October 1835.

Register No. 386 R Turnbull CC
W. Meredith JP

Brunswick County Court October 26th 1835

The above Certificate was compared with the person of the above MARY MALONE & found to be correct.

R Turnbull

=====

Brunswick County to wit

I do certify that the bearer hereof LYDDIA ROBERTS a free woman of colour five feet four Inches high forty five years old has a scar on the left cheek was emancipated by OWEN MYRICK as appears by the deed of emancipation and is duly Registered in my office. Given under my hand this 28th day of Sept. 1835

R Turnbull CC

Register No. 387
Wm. Meredith JP

Brunswick County Court Sept. 28th 1835

The above Certificate was compared with the persor of the above LIDDIA ROBERTS and found to be correct.

R Turnbull CC

=====

Brunswick County to wit

I do certify that the bearer hereof BEN HARRISON a free man of colour of yellow complexion twenty four years of age five feet six Inches high has a small scar on the right hand below the wrist was born free as appears from the evidence of R H H WALLTON and is duly registered in my office this 23 day of May 1836.

Register No. 388 R Turnbull CC
Jno. Manning JP

Brunswick County Court May 23 1836

The above certificate was compared with the person of the above BEN HARRISON & found to be correct.

R Turnbull CC

=====

Brunswick County to wit

I do certify that the bearer hereof JACKSON STEWART a mulatto twenty two years old, six feet high, has a scar on the forehead between the eyes, and was born free as appears from the evidence of RICHARD H H WALLTON, and is duly registered in my office this 23 day of May 1836.

Register No. 389 R Turnbull CBC
John Manning JP

Brunswick County Court May 23rd 1836

The above certificate was compared with the person of the said JACKSON STEWART and found to be correct.

Teste R Turnbull CBC

=====

Brunswick County to wit

I do certify that the bearer hereof THOMAS STEWART a free man of Colour dark complexion twenty seven years old six feet high has a scar on the little finger of the left hand and also a scar on the back part of the head, was born free as appears from the evidence of R H H WALLTON, and is duly registered in my Office this 23rd day of May 1836.

Register No. 390 R Turnbull CBC
Wm Meredith

Brunswick County Court 23 May 1836

The above certificate was compared with the person of the said THOMAS STEWART and found to be correct.

Teste R Turnbull CBC

=====

Brunswick County to wit

I do hereby Certify that the PATRICK STEWART a free man of dark complexion twenty three years old five feet ten inches high has a scar on the chin was born free as appears from the evidence of R H H WALLTON, and is duly registered in my office this 23 day of May 1836.

Register No. 391 R Turnbull CC
Wm. Meredith JP

Brunswick County Court May 23 1836

The above certificate was compared with the person of the above PATRICK STEWART & found to be correct.

Teste R Turnbull CC

=====

Brunswick County to wit

I do hereby Certify that the bearer hereof JOE ATKINS a free man of color dark complexion five feet 10½ Inches high about 22 years old has a scar on the right thumb was born free as appears from the evidence of BENJA. PHIPPS, and is duly registered in my office. Given under my hand this 22nd day of August AD 1836.

Register No. 392 R Turnbull CC
Wm Meredith JP

Brunswick County Court August Term 1836
The above Certificate was compared with the person of the said JOE ATKINS & found to be correct.

Teste R Turnbull CC

=====

(Note: At this point the scribe began to number the registers one hundred less. The number following 392 is 293, etc. The book continues with this numbering through 358 when he again jumps one hundred to 459. Duplicate numbers will carry an asterisk, i. e., 293, 294*, . . . 358*, 459, 460, . . . 551.)*

=====

Brunswick County to wit

I do hereby Certify that the bearer hereof MARTHA ATKINS a free woman of color five feet two Inches high eighteen years old has a scar on the nose was born free as appears from the evidence of BENJA PHIPPS and is duly registered in my office. Given under my hand this 22 August 1836.

Register No. 293* R Turnbull CC
Wm Meredith JP

Brunswick County Court AUGUST Term 1836
The above certificate was compared with the person of the said MARTHA ATKINS & found to be correct.

R Turnbull CC

=====

Brunswick County to wit

I do hereby certify that the bearer hereof MILLEY EDMUNDS a free woman of Colour five feet one inch high 22 years of age was bron free as appears from the evidence of WM. LOW SMITH and is duly registered in my office this 22nd day of August 1836.

Register No. 294* R Turnbull
Benja D Chapman

Brunswick County Court August Term 1836
The above certificate was compared with the person of the said MILLEY EDMUNDS & found to be correct.

R Turnbull CC

=====

Brunswick County to wit
I do hereby certify that the bearer hereof PEGGY EDMUNDS a free woman of Colour dark complexion forty years old about five feet & 1½ high has no scar or mark on head face or hands was emancipated by GRAY EDMUNDS as appears from a former certificate, and is duly registered in my office. Given under my hand this 22nd day of August 1836.

Register 295*
Benja D Chapman
Brunswick County Court August Term 1836
The above certificate was compared with the person of the said PEGGY EDMUNDS and found to be correct.
Teste R Turnbull CC

=====

Brunswick County to wit
I do certify that the bearer hereof PASCAL STEWART a free man of colour 22 years of age five feet 10 inches high has a scar on the right eye was born (sic) as appears from the evidence of R H H WALLTON and is duly registered in my office. Given under my hand this 23rd day of May 1836.

Register 296*
Wm. Meredith JP

Brunswick County Court August Term 1836
The above certificate was compared with the person of the said PASCAL STEWART and found to be correct.
Teste R Turnbull CC

=====

Brunswick County to wit
I do certify that the bearer hereof DEMPSEY EASTER a freeman of Colour fifty years old six feet high has a scar on the left wrist was emancipated by OWEN MYRICK and is duly registered in my office. Given under my hand this 23 day of May 1836.

Register No. 297* R Turnbull
Benja. D. Chapman JP
Brunswick County Court May Term 1836
The above certificate was compared with the person of the said DEMSEY EASTER and found to be correct.
Teste R Turnbull CC

=====

Brunswick County to wit

I do certify that the bearer hereof AUSTIN ROBBINS a free man of Colour about fifty eight years old five feet seven Inches high has a scar on the right jaw, no other scar on his face, head or hands, was emancipated by EDW'D DROMGOOLE Sen. as appears from a former certificate duly recorded. Given under my hand this 24th October 1836.

Register No. 298* R Turnbull CC
Jno. Wyche JP

=====

Brunswick County to wit

I do certify that the bearer hereof ABRAHAM BOATSWAIN a free man of Colour about sixty nine years of age five feet five Inches and an half high has a small scar on the under lip and on his right hand has a small scar from a burn was emancipated by EDWARD DROMGOOLE Sen. as appears from a former certificate duly Recorded. Given under my hand this 24th October 1836.

Register 299* R Turnbull CC
John Wyche JP

Brunswick Court Oct. Term 1836
The above certificates were compared with the persons of the said ROBBINS and BOATSWAIN and found to be correct.

Teste R Turnbull CC

=====

Brunswick County to wit

I do hereby certify that the bearer hereof Twenty one years of age, CARGILL OWEN, mulatto five feet eight Inches and a half high, has a scar at the corner of the right eye, a scar over the left eye, on the edge of the eye brow, and scar on the lower part of the fore finger of the left hand, was born free. Given under my hand this 23r day of December 1837

Register No. 300* Teste R Turnbull CBC

Brunswick County Court December Term 1837
The above Certificate was compared with the person of the said CARGILL OWEN and found to be correct.

Teste R Turnbull CC

=====

Brunswick County to wit

I do hereby certify that the bearer hereof TRAVIS PELHAM a free man of Color dark complexion five feet eight Inches high twenty two years of age, was born free as appears from the Testimony of R H H WALLTON and is duly registered in my office. Given under my hand this 27th day of March 1837.

Register No. 301* R Turnbull CBC
John Manning

Brunswick County Court March Term 1837
The above certificate was compared with the person of the said TRAVIS PELHAM and found to be correct.

Teste R Turnbull CC

=====

Brunswick County to wit

I do hereby Certify that the WILLIAM MASON a free man of Color yellow Complexion five feet seven Inches high twenty four years of age was born free as appears from the Evidence of JOHN C JONES and is duly registered in my Office. Given under my hand this 27th day of March 1837.

Register No. 302* R Turnbull CC
Burwell B Wilkes

Brunswick County Court March Term 1837
The above Certificate was compared with the person of the said WILLIAM MASON and found to be correct.

Teste R Turnbull CC

=====

Brunswick County to wit

I do hereby Certify that the bearer hereof JULIUS STEWART a free man of Color Dark complexion five feet eleven Inches and three quarters high, thirty nine years of age, scar on the nose between the eyes was born free as appears from the Evidence of R H H WALLTON, and is duly registered in my Office.

Register No. 303* R Turnbull CC
F W Green JP

Brunswick County Court May Term 1837
The above certificate was compared with the person of the said JULIUS STEWART and found to be correct.

Teste R Turnbull CC

=====

Brunswick County to wit

I do certify that the bearer hereof RICHARD OWEN a free man of Colour about twenty seven years of age five feet ten and an half Inches high has several small scars on the back of each hand, another on the left thumb and one over the right eye was born free as appears by the evidence of EDW C SMITH and is duly registered in my office this 28th day of May 1832

Register No. 304* R Turnbull CC
Rob't. Jackson

Brunswick County Court May Term 1832
The above certificate was compared with the person of the said RICHARD OWEN and found to be correct.

Teste R Turnbull CC

=====

Brunswick County to wit

I do hereby certify that the bearer FANNY COLEMAN a free woman of Colour (mulatto) about thirty years of age no Scar or mark on face hands or head is one of the Children of CATY who recovered her freedom in the late Superior Court of Brunswick County five feet five Inches and a half and is duly registered in my Office. Given under my hand this 24th day of April 1837.

Register No. 305* R Turnbull CBC
Benjamin D Chapman

Brunswick County Court April Term 1837
The above certificate was compared with the person of the said FANNY COLEMAN and found to be correct.

Teste R Turnbull CC

=====

Brunswick County to wit

I do hereby certify that the bearer hereof THOS. COLEMAN a free man of Colour yellow Complexion twenty three years of age five feet Six Inches and a half high, has a small scar under the right eye is one of the Children of CATY who recovered her freedom in the late Superior Court of Law of said County and is duly registered in my Office. Given under my hand this 24th day of April 1837.

Register No. 306* R Turnbull CBC
Benjamin D Chapman

Brunswick County Court April Term 1837
The above certificate was compared with the person of the said THOMAS COLEMAN & found to be correct.

Teste R Turnbull CC

=====

Brunswick County to wit
I do hereby Certify that the bearer hereof JOHN E EASTER a free man of Color yellow complexion twenty one years of age five feet six Inches and a half has a scar over the right eye scar on the left nostrile was born free as appears from the Testimony of R H H WALLTON and is duly Registered in my office this 26th day of June 1837

Register No. 307* R Turnbull CC
Wm. Meredith JP
Brunswick County Court June Term 1837
The above Certificate was compared with the person of the said JOHN E EASTER and found to be correct.
Teste R Turnbull CC

=====

Brunswick County to wit
I do hereby Certify that the bearer hereof ALFRED MERRITT a free man of Color twenty three years of age Dark complexion five feet eight inches high no scar was born free as appears from the Testimony of BENJA D CHAPMAN and is duly registered in my office this 26th day of June 1837

Register No. 308* R Turnbull CC
Wm Meredith JP
Brunswick County Court June Term 1837
The above Certificate was compared with the person of the said JOHN E EASTER and found to be correct.
Teste R Turnbull CC

=====

Brunswick County to wit
I do hereby Certify that the bearer hereof ANDERSON EASTER a free man of Color yellow complexion twenty one years of age five feet nine Inches and a half high Scar on the right hand was born free as appears from the Testimony of R H H WALLTON and is duly registered in my office this 26th day of June 1837.

Register No. 309* R Turnbull CC
Wm. Meredith JP
Brunswick County Court June Term 1837
The above Certificate was compared with the person of the said ANDERSON EASTER and found to be correct.
Teste R Turnbull CC

=====

Brunswick County to wit

I do hereby Certify that the bearer hereof ISAAC WALKER a free man of colour Dark complexion five feet eight inches and an half high has a scar on the left wrist one above the right eye and a wen on the Top of the forehead on the right side was emancipated by the Will of WILLIAM WALKER dec'd and is fifty four years of age and is duly registered in my office. Given under my hand this 26th day of June 1837.

Register No. 310* R Turnbull CC

Brunswick County Court July Term 1837

The above Certificate was compared with the person of the said IS AC WALKER and found to be correct.

Teste R Turnbull CC

=====

Brunswick County to wit

I do hereby certify that the bearer hereof EMMA ATKINS a free woman of Colour about twenty five years of age, scar on fore finger left hand, was emancipated by OWEN MYRICK, as appears from the evidence of R H H WALLTON and is duly registered in my office this 28 day of August 1837

Register 311* R Turnbull CBC

Brunswick Court August Term 1837

The above certificate was compared with the person of the said EMMA ATKINS and found to be correct.

Teste R Turnbull CBC

=====

Brunswick County to wit

I do certify that the bearer hereof OSBORNE (BOYKIN) VICK a free man of colour Dark complexion about thirty four years of age five feet five inches high has no mark or Scar on the face head or hands, was born free as appears from a former Certificate. Given under my hand this 26th day of February 1838.

Register (312)* R Turnbull CBC

Brunswick County Court February Term 1838

The above Certificate was compared with the person of the said OS-BORNE (BOYKIN) VICK and found to be correct.

Teste R Turnbull CBC

=====

Brunswick County to wit
I do hereby Certify that the bearer hereof JOSEPH CAIN a free man of colour Dark complexion about thirty years of age five feet eight inches and a half high has no Mark or scar on the face head or hands, was born free as appears from the evidence of F W GREEN and is duly registered in my office this 26th day of Feby. 1838

Register No. 313* R Turnbull CBC

Brunswick County Court February Ferm 1838

The above Certificate was compared with the person of the said JOSEPH CAIN and found to be correct.

Teste R Turnbull CC

=====

Brunswick County to wit
I do hereby Certify that the bearer hereof RANSOM ROBERTS a free man of colour Dark complexion about twenty three years of age five feet nine Inches high has no mark or Scar on the face head or hands was born free as appears from the evidence of RICHARD H H WALL-TON and is duly registered in my office this 26th day of March 1838

Register No. 314* R Turnbull CC

Wm A E Merritt JP

Brunswick County Court March Term 1838

The above certificate was compared with the person of the said RANSOM ROBERTS and found to be correct.

Teste R Turnbull CC

=====

Brunswick County to wit
I do hereby Certify that the bearer hereof POLLY SMITH a free woman of colour yellow complexion about Forty seven years of age five feet four Inches and a half high has no mark or Scar on the face head or hands was born free as appears from the evidence of GEORGE WALKER and is duly registered in my Office this 26th day of March 1838

Register No. 315* R Turnbull CBC

John Tucker JP

Brunswick County Court March Term 1838

The above Certificate was compared with the person of the said POLLY SMITH and found to be correct.

Teste R Turnbull CBC

=====

Brunswick County to wit
I do hereby Certify that the bearer hereof ELIJAH SMITH a free man of colour Brown complexion about twenty three years of age five feet eleven Inches high has no mark or Scar on the face head or hands was born free as appears from the evidence of GEORGE WALKER and is duly Registered in my Office this 26th day of March 1838.

Register No. 316* R Turnbull CBC
John Tucker JP
Brunswick County Court March Term 1838
The above Certificate was compared with the person of the said ELIJAH SMITH and found to be correct.
Teste R Turnbull CBC

=====

Brunswick County to wit
I do hereby Certify that the bearer hereof GINSEY SMITH a free woman of colour yellow complexion about thirty one years of age five feet two Inches high has no mark or Scar on the face head or hands was born free as appears from the evidence of GEORGE WALKER and is duly registered in my Office this 26th day of March 1838

Register No. 317* R Turnbull CBC
John Tucker JP
Brunswick County Court March Term 1838
The above Certificate was compared with the person of the said GINSEY SMITH and found to be correct.
Teste R Turnbull CBC

=====

Brunswick County to wit
I hereby Certify that WM D KENNEDY a free man of Dark Complexion, five feet eight Inches high about thirty eight years of age has no Scar on face head or hands was born free as appears by an order of the Hustings Court of Richmond. Given under my hand this 28th day of May 1838

Registered No. 318* R Turnbull CBC
John Wyche
Brunswick County Court May Term 1838
The above Certificate was compared with the person of the said WM D KENNEDY and found to be correct.
Teste R Turnbull CBC

=====

Brunswick County to wit

I do hereby Certify that CHARLES ROBERTS a free man of yellow complexion, five feet eight Inches high has a scar on his forehead, and one immediately under his right ear occasioned by burns, about thirty five years of age and was born free as appears from a former Certificate. Given under my hand this 23rd day of July 1838

Register No. 319* R Turnbull CC
F W Green JP

Brunswick County Court July Term 1838
The above Certificate was compared with the person of the said CHARLES ROBERTS and found to be correct.

Teste R Turnbull CC

=====

Brunswick County to wit

I do hereby Certify that the bearer hereof JOHN CAIN a free man of Dark complexion five feet six Inches high twenty one years old was born free as appears from the evidence of F W GREEN And is duly registered in my Office. Given under my hand this 27th day of August 1838

Register No. 320* R Turnbull CC
Hiram H Blick JP

Brunswick County Court August Term 1838
The above Certificate was compared with the person of the said JOHN CAIN and found to be correct.

R Turnbull CBC

=====

Brunswick County to wit

I do Certify that the bearer hereof HANNAH HARRISON (mulatto) four feet Eleven Inches high, thirty two years of age, has no scar on face head or hands, was born free as appears from the evidnece of ___________ and is duly registered in my Office. Given under my hand this ______ day of __________ 1838.

Register No. 321* R Turnbull CC

Brunswick County Court _________ Term 1838
The above Certificate was compared with the person of the said HANNAH HARRISON and found to be correct.

Teste R Turnbull CC

=====

Brunswick County to wit

I do Certify that the bearer hereof NANCY HARRISON a free woman of colour (mulatto) five feet one fourth of an Inch high about fifty seven years of age, has a scar on the left side of her forehead was born free as appears from the evidence of ______and is duly registered in my office. Given under my hand this_____day of _____1838.

Register No. 322* R Turnbull CC

Brunswick County Court ________Term 1838

The above Certificate was compared with the person of the said NANCY HARRISON & found to be correct.

Teste R Turnbull CBC

=====

Brunswick County to wit

I do certify that the bearer hereof LUCY GRAIN a free woman of Colour yellow complexion five feet one Inch high about twenty one years of Age has no scar on face head or hands was born free as appears from the evidence of R H H WALLTON and is duly registered in my Office. Given under my hands this 22 day of October 1838

No. 323* Teste R Turnbull CBC

Brunswick County Court 22 October 1838

The above Certificate was compared by the Court with the person of the said LUCY GRAIN and found to be correct.

Teste R Turnbull CBC

=====

Brunswick County to wit

I do hereby Certify that the bearer hereof RUFFIN STEWART a free man of color yellow complexion five feet Eleven Inches and a half high about twenty two years of age has no scar on face head or hands was born free as appears from the evidence of A CLAIBORNE and is duly registered in my Office. Given under my hand this 27th day of November 1838.

Register No. 324* Teste R Turnbull CC

Brunswick County Court November Term 1838

The above Certificate was compared by the Court with the person of the said RUFFIN STEWART & found to be correct.

Teste R Turnbull CC

=====

Brunswick County to wit
I do hereby Certify that the bearer hereof PATRICK STEWART a free man of color yellow complexion six feet high about twenty four years of age has no scar on face head or hands was born free as appears from the evidence of AUGUSTINE CLAIBORNE and is duly registered in my Office. Given under my hand this 26th day of November 1838.

Register No. 325* Teste R Turnbull CC
Wm Meredith JP

Brunswick County Court November Term 1838
The above Certificate was compared by the Court with the person of the said STEWART and found to be correct.

Teste R Turnbull CC

=====

Brunswick County to wit
I do Certify that the bearer hereof QUEEN EASTER a free woman of color yellow complexion five feet three Inches high about twenty one years of age has a scar on the right Rist was born free as appears from the evidence of JESSE KELLY and is duly registered in my Office. Given under my hand this 26th day of November 1838.

No. 326* Teste R Turnbull CC
Benjamin D Chapman

Brunswick County Court November Term 1838
The above Certificate was compared by the Court with the person of the said EASTER and found to be correct.

Teste R Turnbull CBC

=====

Brunswick County to wit
I do Certify that the bearer hereof CLAIBORNE EASTER a free man of color, five feet eleven Inches high twenty one years of age has no scar on face head or hands was born free as appears from the evidence of F W GREEN and is duly registered in my Office. Given under my hand this 28th day of Jany. 1839.

Register No. 327* R Turnbull CBC
E R Tucker JP

Brunswick County Court January Term 1839
The above Certificate was compared by the Court with the person of the said CLAIBORNE EASTER and found to be correct.

Teste R Turnbull CBC

=====

Brunswick County to wit
I do Certify that the bearer hereof FANNY MERRITT a free woman of color Dark complexion five feet two Inches and a half high about twenty nine years of age has a scar over the left eye was born free as appears from the evidence of R H H WALLTON and is duly registered in my office. Given under my hand this 22nd day of October 1838

Register No. 328* R Turnbull CC
W B Meredith JP
Brunswick County Court October Term 1838
The above Certificate was compared by the Court with the person of said MERRITT and found to be correct.
Teste R Turnbull CC

=====

Brunswick County to wit
I do Certify that the bearer hereof FANNY EASTER a free woman of colour yellow complexion five feet six Inches high about twenty years of age has no scar on face head or hands was born free as appears from the evidence of JESSE KELLY and is duly registered in my office. Given under my hand this 26th day of Nov. 1838

Register No. 329* Teste R Turnbull CC
Benjamin D Chapman JP
Brunswick County Court November Term 1838
The above Certificate was compared by the Court with the person of the said EASTER and found to be correct.
Teste R Turnbull CC

=====

Brunswick County to wit
I do Certify that the bearer hereof HICKS GRAIN a free man of color dark complexion five feet five Inches high about thirty one years of age has no scar on face head or hands was born free as appears from a former Certificate. Given under my hand this 28th day of January 1839

Register No. 330* Teste R Turnbull CC
Edwd B Tucker JP
Brunswick County Court January Term 1839
The above certificate was compared by the Court with the person of the said GRAIN and found to be correct.
Teste R Turnbull CC

=====

Brunswick County to wit
I do Certify that the bearer hereof CATHARINE CHAPMAN a free woman of color five feet two Inches high twenty four years of age has no scar on face head or hands was born free as appears from the evidence of F W GREEN and is duly registered in my Office. Given under my hand this 28th day of Jany 1839

Register No. 331* R Turnbull CC
Edwd B Tucker JP
Brunswick County Court January Term 1839
The above Certificate was compared by the Court with the person of the said CHAPMAN and found to be correct.
Teste R Turnbull CC

=====

Brunswick County to wit
I do Certify that the bearer hereof MARTHA CHAPMAN a free woman of color Brown complexion four feet eleven Inches and a half high about twenty years of age, has no scar on face head or hands was born free as appears from the evidence of F W GREEN and is duly registered in my Office. Given under my hand this 28th day of Jany. 1839

Register No. 332* R Turnbull CC
Edwd B Tucker JP
Brunswick County Court Jany 1839
The above Certificate was compared by the Court with the person of the said CHAPMAN and found to be correct.
Teste R Turnbull CC

=====

Brunswick County to wit
I do Certify that the bearer hereof MARY JANE ROBERTS a free woman of yellow complexion about twenty years of age five feet one Inch high has no scar on face head or hands was born free as appears from the evidence of F W GREEN and is duly registered in my office. Given under my hand this 28th day of January 1839

Register No. 333* R Turnbull CC
Edwd B Tucker JP
Brunswick County Court January Term 1839
The above Certificate was compared by the Court with the person of the said ROBERTS and found to be correct.
Teste R Turnbull CC

=====

Brunswick County to wit
I do Certify that the bearer hereof FANNY STEWART a free woman of color (mulatto) about twenty one years of age five feet six Inches high has a scar on the right side of her forehead was born free as appears from the evidence of F W GREEN and is duly registered in my office this 28th day of January 1839.

Register No. 334* R Turnbull CC
Edwd B Tucker
Brunswick County Court Jany Term 1839
The above Certificate was compared by the Court with the person of the said STEWART and found to be correct.
Teste R Turnbull CC

=====

Brunswick County to wit
I do hereby Certify that the bearer hereof RACHEL CAIN a free woman of Color yellow complexion five feet two Inches and a hal high has no scar on face head or hands about twenty three years was born free as appears from the evidence of F W GREEN and is duly registered in my office. Given under my hand this 28 day of Jany. 1839

Register No. 334* R Turnbull CC
Edwd. B. Tucker JP
Brunswick County Court Jany Term 1839
The above Certificate was compared by the Court with the person of the said CAIN and found to be correct.
Teste R Turnbull CC

=====

Brunswick County to wit
I do Certify that the bearer hereof CATHARINE PELHAM a free woman of color Dark complexion about twenty one years of age five feet high has no scar on face head or hands was born free as appears from the evidence of R H H WALLTON and is duly registered in my office this 24th day of June 1839.

Register No. 334* R Turnbull CBC
Isham Trotter JP
Brunswick County Court June Term 1839
The above Certificate was compared by the Court with the person of the said CATHARINE PARHAM & found to be correct.
Teste R Turnbull CC

=====

Brunswick County to wit
I do hereby Certify that the bearer hereof WINFREE B F STEWART, a free man of yellow complexion about twenty eight years of age, six feet two Inches and a half high, has a small scar near the right (sic) occasioned by a burn, one in the Palm of his left hand and one of the fingers of his right hand swelled at the end, occasioned by its having been broken and no other perceivable was born free as appears from a former Certificate and is duly registered in my Office this 24th day of June 1839

Register No. 335* Teste R Turnbull CC
J C Jones JP
Brunswick County Court June Term 1839
The above Certificate was compared by the Court with the person of the said STEWART & found to be correct.
Teste R Turnbull CC

=====

Brunswick County to wit
I do hereby Certify that THOS EASTER a free man of color Dark complexion five feet seven Inches and a half high, about twenty one years of Age, has a Scar on his left Thumb and on back of his left hand near the thumb, was born free as appears from the evidence of F. W. GREEN and is duly Registered in my Office this 26th day of August 1839.

F W Green JP Teste R Turnbull CBC
Register No. 336*
Brunswick County Court August Term 1839
The above Certificate was compared by the Court with the person of the said EASTER and found to be correct.
Teste R Turnbull CBC

=====

Brunswick County to wit
I do hereby Certify that the bearer hereof WATKINS JONES a free man of color Dark complexion about twenty one years of age five feet eight Inches high has no Scar on face head or hands was born free as appears from the evidence of RICHARD BIGGS and is duly registered in my Office this 23 day of Sept. 1839.

Register No. 337* R Turnbull CC
Robt R Jones JP
Brunswick County Court September Term 1839
The above Certificate was compared by the Court with the person of the said JONES & found to be correct.
Teste R Turnbull CC

=====

Brunswick County to wit

I do Certify that the bearer hereof LIZZY ROBERTS a free woman of Color Dark complexion five feet high, has a Scar on her left Thumb, about thirty three years of age was born free as appears from the evidence of BENJAMIN GREEN and is duly registered in my Office this 22nd day of April 1839.

Register No. 338* R Turnbull CBC
Robert R Jones

Brunswick County Court September Term 1839
The above Certificate was compared by the Court with the person of the said LIZZY ROBERTS and found to be correct.
Teste R Turnbull CC

=====

Brunswick County to wit

I do hereby Certify that the bearer hereof REBECCA STEWART a free person of color yellow complexion about forty five years of age five feet six Inches high, has no Scar on face head or hands was born free as appears from the evidence of GEORGE STONE and duly registered in my Office this 23rd day of September 1839.

Register No. 339* R Turnbull CBC
Robt R Jones

Brunswick County Court September Term 1839
The above Certificate was compared by the Court with the person of the said STEWART and found to be correct.
Teste R Turnbull CBC

=====

Brunswick County to wit

I do hereby Certify that the bearer hereof MARTHA STEWART a free person of color (mulatto) about twenty two years of age five feet five Inches and a half high, has a Scar over her right eye, and on her right Thumb was born free as appears from the evidence of GEORGE STONE and is duly registered in my Office this 23rd day of September 1839.

Register No. 340* R Turnbull CC
Robt R Jones

Brunswick County Court September Term 1839
The above Certificate was compared by the Court with the person of the said STEWART & found to be correct.
Teste R Turnbull CBC

=====

Brunswick County to wit
I do hereby Certify that the bearer hereof WILLIAM WALKER a free man of color, Dark compelxion twenty one years of age, has two small scars on the back of his right hand, and one on his nose, five feet ten Inches high was born free as appears from the evidence of ISHAM TROTTER and is duly registered in my Office this 28th day of Oct. 1839

Register No. 341* R Turnbull CBC
Wm Meredith
Brunswick County Court Oct. Term 1839
The above Certificate was compared by the Court with the person of the said WALKER and found to be correct.
Teste R Turnbull CC

=====

Brunswick County to wit
I do hereby Certify that the bearer hereof ANN WALKER a free woman of color, about twenty six years of age, five feet five Inches high, has no Scar on face head or hands, was born free as appears from the evidence of ISHAM TROTTER and is duly registered in my Office this 28th day of Oct. 1839.

Register No. 342* R Turnbull CBC
Wm Meredith JP
Brunswick County Court Oct. Term 1839
The above Certificate was compard by the Court with the person of the said WALKER and found to be correct.
Teste R Turnbull CBC

=====

Brunswick County, to wit,
I do hereby Certify that the bearer hereof ALBERT MALONE, a free man of color, Dark complexion about twenty three years of age, five feet six Inches and a half high, has a small scar between the forefinger and thumb of the right hand was born free as appears from the evidence of F W GREEN and is duly registered in my Office this 28th day of Oct. 1839.

Register No. 343* R Turnbull CBC
Wm. Meredith JP
Brunswick County Court Oct. Term 1839
The above Certificate was compared by the Court with the person of the said MALONE and found to be correct.
Teste R Turnbull CBC

=====

Brunswick County, to wit,
I do hereby Certify that the bearer hereof WILLIAM MALONE a free man of color Dark complexion about twenty one years of age, five feet nine Inches high, has a scar on the back of his left hand, and one on his forehead, was born free as appears from the evidence of F W GREEN and is duly registered in my office this 28th day of Oct. 1839.

Register No. 344* R Turnbull CBC
Wm. Meredith JP
Brunswick County Court Oct. Term 1839
The above Certificate was compared by the Court with the person of the said MALONE and found to be correct.
Teste R Turnbull CBC

=====

Brunswick County to wit
I do hereby Certify that the bearer hereof JINSEY STEWART a free woman of color Dark complexion about 38 years of age five feet three Inches high, has no Scar on face head or hands was born free as appears from the evidence of F W GREEN and is duly registered in my Office this 24th day of February 1840.

R H H Wallton Chs. Turnbull CBC
Register No. 345*
Brunswick County Court February Term 1840
The above certificate was compared by the Court with the person of the said STEWART and found to be correct.
Teste Chs. Turnbull CBC

=====

Brunswick County, to wit,
I do hereby certify that the bearer hereof LITTLETON STEWART a free person of color Dark complexion about thirty six years of age six feet two Inches high, has a scar on the back of his left hand was born free as appears from the evidence of F. W. GREEN and is duly registered in my Office this 24th day of February 1840.

R H H Wallton Chs. Turnbull CBC
Register No. 346*
Brunswick County Court February Term 1840
The above Certificate was compared by the Court with the person of the said LITTLETON STEWART & found to be correct.
Teste Chs. Turnbull CBC

=====

Brunswick County to wit

I do hereby certify that the bearer hereof ROBERT EASTER a free person of color Dark complexion about twenty one years of age five feet eight Inches high has a scar over his left eye was born free as appears from the evidence of F W GREEN and is duly registered in my Office this 24th day of Feby 1840

Register No. 347* Chs. Turnbull CC
R H H Wallton JP

Brunswick County Court Feby Term 1840

The above certificate was compared by the Court with the person of the said EASTER & found to be correct.

Teste Chs. Turnbull CC

=====

Brunswick County, to wit,

I do hereby certify that the bearer hereof BOB MALONE a free man of color Dark complexion about twenty six years of age, five feet nine Inches has two small scars over the right eye was born free as appears from the evidence of WM B WILKINSON and is duly registered in my Office this 9th day of October 1839

Register No. 348* R Turnbull CC
Wm Meredith JP

Brunswick County Court October Term 1839

The above Certificate was compared by the Court with the person of the said MALONE & found to be correct.

Teste R Turnbull

=====

Brunswick County to wit

I do hereby certify that the bearer hereof SALLY OWEN a free woman of yellow complexion about twenty six years of age five feet 3 Inches high has a scar on the left forefinger one on the back of the left hand & one on the left side of her left eye was born free as appears from the Evidence of EDWD C SMITH & is duly registered in my office this 28th day of October 1839

Register No. 349* R Turnbull CC
Wm Meredith JP

Brunswick County Court October Term 1839

The above Certificate was compared with the person of the said SALLY OWEN & found to be correct.

Teste R Turnbull CC

=====

Brunswick County to wit
I do hereby Certify that the bearer hereof HANNAH HARRISON a free person of color (mulatto) about thirty seven years of age, five feet one Inch high has a scar on the back of her left hand was born free as appears from the evidence of ALEX MALLORY and is duly registered in my Office this 28th day of October 1839.

Registered No. 350* R Turnbull CC
Wm Meredith JP

Brunswick County Court October Term 1839
The above Certificate was compared with the person of the said HANNAH HARRISON & found to be correct.

Teste R Turnbull CC

=====

Brunswick County to wit
I do hereby Certify that the bearer hereof HARRY HARRISON a free man of color yellow complexion about forty years of age five feet Eleven Inches high has no scar on face head or hands, was born free as appears from the evidence of E. C. SMITH, and is duly registered in my office this 26th day of August 1839

Register No. 351* R Turnbull CC
John Wyche JP

Brunswick County Court August Term 1839
The above certificate was compared with the person of the said HARRY HARRISON & found to be correct.

Teste R Turnbull CC

=====

Brunswick County, to wit:
I do hereby Certify that the bearer hereof JAMES WOODLEY a free man of colour five feet eight inches and a half high has a Scar on his forehead Dark complexion was born free as appears from the evidence of G. C. DROMGOOLE and is duly registered in my Office this 28 day of Sept. 1840.

Register No. 352* Chs. Turnbull CC
Burwell B Wilkes JP

Brunswick County Court September Term 1840
The above certificate was compared by the Court with the said WOODLEY and found to be correct.

Teste Chs. Turnbull CC

=====

Brunswick County to wit
I do hereby Certify that the bearer hereof DENISON STEWART a free person of colour Dark complexion about twenty two years of age, five feet eleven inches and a half high has a scar on his right wrist and one over his right eye, was born free as appears from the evidence of F. W. GREEN and is duly registered in my office this 26 day of October 1840.

Register No. 353* Chs. Turnbull CBC
Burwell B Wilkes
Brunswick County Court October Term 1840
The above certificate was compared by the court with the person of the said STEWART and found to be correct.
Teste Chs.Turnbull CC

=====

Brunswick County, to wit
I do hereby certify that the bearer hereof SUSAN JACKSON a free woman of color mulatto about nineteen years of age five feet four Inches high has a scar on the back of her left hand was born free as appears from the evidence of F W GREEN and is duly registered in my Office this 24th day of Feby 1840.

Register No. 354* Chs. Turnbull CC
R H H Wallton JP
Brunswick County Court Feby Term 1840
The within Certificate was compared by the Court with the person of the said SUSAN JACKSON and found to be correct.
Teste Chs. Turnbull CBC

=====

Brunswick County, to wit,
I hereby certify that the bearer hereof WILLIAM POMPEY a free person of colour, yellow complexion, about twenty one years of age, five feet three inches and a half high, has no scar on face, head or hands, was born free as appears from the evidence of GEORGE STONE and is duly registered in my Office this 28th day of December 1840.

Register No. 355* Chs. Turnbull CC
D Hicks JP
Brunswick County Court December Term 1840
The above certificate was compared by the court with the person of the said POMPEY and found to be correct.
Teste Chs. Turnbull CBC

=====

Brunswick County to wit:
I do hereby certify, that the bearer hereof BETSEY STEWART a free person of colour yellow complexion, about twenty five years of age, five feet three inches high, has no scar on face, head or hands was born free as appears from the evidence of GEO. STONE and is duly registered in my Office this 22nd day of MARCH 1841.

Register No. 356* Chs. Turnbull
John C Jones JP
Brunswick County Court March Term 1841
The above certificate was compared by the court with the person of the said STEWART and found to be correct.
Teste Chs. Turnbull CC

=====

Brunswick County to wit
I hereby certify that the bearer hereof JAMES MERRITT a free person of colour yellow complexion twenty one years of age five feet nine inches & a half high has no scar on face head or hands was born free as appears from the evidence of THOMAS T. KING and is duly Registered in my Office this 26 day of April 1841.

Register No. 357* Chs. Turnbull CC
John P. Atkinson JP
Brunswick County Court April Term 1841
The above certificate was compared by the Court with the person of the sd. JAMES MERRITT and found to be correct.
Teste Chs. Turnbull CC

=====

Brunswick County to wit
I hereby certify that the bearer hereof WILLIAM MERRITT a free person of collow dark complexion twenty one years of age six feet high has a scar on the thumb and forefinger of the left hand was born free as appears from the evidence of F W GREEN and is duly registered in my office this 15 day of May 1841.

Robt R Jones JP Chs. Turnbull CC
Register No. 358*
Brunswick County Court May Term 1841
The above certificate was compared by the court with the person of the sd. WILLIAM MERRITT & found to be correct.
Teste Charles Turnbull CC

=====

Brunswick County to wit

I do hereby certify that the bearer hereof HEROD MALONE of (sic) free man of color Dark Complexion about twenty three years of age five feet five inches & a half high has a Scar on the little finger of the left hand occasioned by a burn was born free as appears from the evidence of WM B WILKINSON and is duly Registered in my Office. this 25 day of May 1840

Register No. 459 Teste Chs. Turnbull CC
John Tucker JP

Brunswick County Court May term 1840

The above certificate was compared by the court with the person of the said HEROD MALONE & found to be correct.

Teste Charles Turnbull CC

=====

Brunswick County to wit

I hereby certify that the bearer hereof AMY PELHAM a free person of colour dark complexion about twenty years of age five feet one inch high has no scar on face head or hands was born free as appears from the evidence of R H H WALLTON and is duly registered in my office this 28 day of June 1841.

J A Riddick Chs. Turnbull CC
Register No. 460

Brunswick County Court June term 1841

The above certificate was compared by the court with the person of the sd. AMY PELHAM & found to be correct.

Teste Charles Turnbull CC

=====

Brunswick County to wit

I do hereby certify that the bearer hereof DAVID EDMUNDS a free person of colour dark complexion twenty one years of age, five feet four inches and a half has a Scar on the back of his right hand one on his right wrist and one on the left side of his forehead, was born free as appears from the evidence of JOHN DUGGER and is duly registered in my office this 26 July 1841.

Register No. 461 Charles Turnbull CC
John Wyche

Brunswick County Court November term 1841

The above certificate was compared by the court with the person of the said DAVID EDMUNDS & found to be correct.

Teste Charles Turnbull CC

=====

Brunswick County to wit

I do hereby certify that the bearer hereof POLLY MERRITT a free person of colour dark complexion about thirty years of age five feet eight inches high has no scar on face head or hands was born free as appears from the evidence of F W GREEN and is duly registered in my office this 28 day of Febry 1842.

Register No. 462 Charles Turnbull CC
John Wyche

Brunswick County Court Febry term 1842
The above certificate was compared by the court with the person of the said POLLY MERRITT and found to be correct.

Teste Chs. Turnbull CC

=====

Brunswick County to wit

I do hereby certify that the bearer hereof WILLIAM GILLIS a free person of colour dark complexion about twenty three years of age five feet eight inches and a half high has two scars on the back of his left hand was born free as appears from the evidence of F W GREEN and is duly registered in my offis this 28th day of Febry 1842

Register No. 463 Charles Turnbull CC
John Wyche

Brunswick County Court Febry term 1842
The above Certificate was Compared by the Court with the person of the said WILLIAM GILLIS and found to be Correct.

Teste Charles Turnbull CC

=====

Brunswick County to wit

I do hereby certify that the bearer hereof GRIFFIN EDMUNDS a free person of color dark complexion five feet one inch and a half high has a scar on the back of his right hand was born free as appea from the evidence of LITTLEBERRY BAUGH about twenty five years of age and is duly registered in my offis this 20th day of November 1841.

Register No. 464 Charles Turnbull CC
John Wyche

Brunswick County Court Febry term 1842
The above Certificate was Compared by the Court with the person of th said GRIFFIN EDMUNDS & found to be Correct.

Teste Charles Turnbull

=====

Brunswick County to wit
I do hereby Certify that the bearer hereof RICHARD MANNING a free person of Color Dark Complexion about twenty one years of age five feet Eleven Inches and a half high has a Scar under his left eye was born free as appears from the evidence of BENJA MOORE and is registered in my office this 22nd day of June 1840

Register No. 465 Charles Turnbull CBC
William Meredith JP
Brunswick County Court June term 1840.
The above Certificate was Compared by the Court with the person of the said RICHARD MANNING and found to be Correct.
Teste Charles Turnbull CBC

=====

Brunswick County to wit
I do hereby Certify that JOHN AMPIE a free person of Color Yellow Complexion forty two years of age five feet nine Inches high has a Scar on the left fore finger (part cut off) was born free as appears from the evidence of R D TURNBULL and is duly registered in my office this 25th day of April 1842

Register No. 466 Charles Turnbull CBC
Wm Meredith JP
Brunswick County Court April term 1842
The above Certificate was Compared by the the (sic) Court with the person of the said JOHN AMPIE & found to be Correct.
T Charles Turnbull CBC

=====

Brunswick County to wit
I do hereby certify that the bearer hereof GEORGE H JONES a free person of color dark complexion about thirty years of age five feet five Inches high has one scar on his chin and one on his left ear (part cut off) was born free as appears from a former Certificate and is duly registered in my Office this 25th day of April 1842

Register No. 467 Charles Turnbull CBC
Burwell B Wilkes
Brunswick County Court April term 1842
The above Certificate was Compared by the Court with the person of the said GEORGE H. JONES & found to be correct.
Teste Charles Turnbull CBC

=====

Brunswick County to wit
I do hereby certify that the bearer hereof BENJAMIN EDMUNDS a free person of Color dark Complexion about twenty Six years of age five feet nine inches high has two scars on his neck below his right ear was born free as appears from the evidence of THOMAS GIBBON & is duly registered in my office this 27th day of June 1842

Benja D Chapman — Charles Turnbull
Register No. 468

Brunswick County Court June term 1842
The above certificate was compared by the Court with the person of BENJA EDMUNDS and found to be correct.

Charles Turnbull CBC

=====

Brunswick County to wit
I do hereby certify that the bearer hereof ROBERTA MOODY a free person of color (Mulatto) about twenty Six years of age five four inches high has a scar on back of right hand was born free as appears from the evidence of R H H WALLTON and is duly registered in my office this 23rd day of May 1842.

Edward B Tucker — Charles Turnbull
Register No. 469

Brunswick County Court May term 1842
The above Certificate was Compared by the Court with the person of the said ROBERTA MOODY and found to be Correct.

Charles Turnbull CBC

=====

Brunswick County to wit
I hereby certify that the bearer hereof CHARLES MERRITT a free person of Colour yellow Complexion about twenty five years of age five feet eight and a half inches high has no Scar on the face hand or head was born free as appears from the evidence of JOHN P ATKINSON and is duly registered in my office this 26th day of Sept. 1842.

Register No. 470 — Chas. Turnbull
R W Field JP

Brunswick County Court Sept term 1842
The above Certificate was Compared by the Court together with the person of the said CHAS. MERRITT and found to be correct.

Chas. Turnbull CBC

=====

Brunswick County to wit
I hereby Certify that the bearer hereof DANIEL ATKINS a free person of Color dark complexion about twenty three years of age one Scar on back of right hand one on back of left hand and one on left wrist five feet nine and a half inches high was born free as appears from the evidence of LEWIS BREWER and is duly registered in my office this 24th day of October 1842.

Register No. 471 Chas. Turnbull
R H H Wallton
Brunswick County Court October term 1842
The above certificate was compared by the Court together with the person of the said DANIEL ATKINS & found to be correct.
Chas. Turnbull CBC

=====

Brunswick County to wit
I hereby certify that the bearer hereof HANSEL MALONE a free person of Colour dark Complexion about twenty four years of age five feet four inches high has a scar on his right wrist one on the back of right hand one on forehead and one over right eye was born free as appears from the evidence of WM B WILKINSON and is duly registered in my office this 27th day of Sept 1842.

Register No. 472 Chas. Turnbull CC
Wm H E Merritt
Brunswick County Court October term 1842
The above Certificate was Compared by the Court with the person of the said HANSEL MALONE and found to be correct.
Teste Charles Turnbull CC

=====

Brunswick County to wit
I hereby Certify that the bearer hereof EMA MALONE a free person of Color, dark Complexion about twenty three years of age, 1 Scar on right wrist, five feet four and a half inches high, was born free as appears from the evidence of WM B WILKINSON and is duly registered in my office this 24th day of Oct. 1842.

Register 473 Chas. Turnbull CC
Wm H E Merritt JP
Brunswick County Court October term
The above Certificate was Compared by the Court with the person of the said EMA MALONE and found to be Correct.
Teste Chas. Turnbull CC

=====

Brunswick County to wit
I do hereby certify that the bearer hereof MARIA EASTE a free person of Color dark Complexion about thirty years of age has two Scars on her right wrist five feet five Inches high was born free as appears from the evidence of R H H WALLTON and is duly registered in my office this 25th Feby 1843.

Register No. 474 Charles Turnbull
B B Wilkes JP
Brunswick County Court Febry term 1843
The above Certificate was compared by the Court with the person of the said MARIA EASTER and found to be correct.
Teste Chas. Turnbull CBC

=====

Brunswick County to wit
I do hereby certify that the bearer hereof CHARLOTTE GRAIN a free person of Color dark Complexion, about forty five years of of (sic) age, five feet three inches high has no Scar on face head or hands was born free as appears from the evidence of R H H WALLTON and is duly registered in my office this 28th day of August 1843.

Register No. 475 E R Turnbull
Wm H E Merritt JP
Brunswick County Court Augt term 1843
The above Certificate was compared by the Court and found to be correct.
Teste E R Turnbull CLK

=====

Brunswick County to wit
I do hereby certify that the bearer hereof ARY MALONE a free person of Color dark Complexion about twenty one years of age five feet five inches high, has one Scar on back of fourth finger of left hand was born free as appears from the evidence of W Y MALLORY and is duly registered in my office this 28th day of August 1843.

Register No. 476 E R Turnbull CLK
Wm H E Merritt JP
Brunswick County Court August term 1843
The above certificate was Compared by the Court with the person of the said ARY MALONE & found to be correct.
Teste E R Turnbull CLK

=====

Brunswick County to wit

I do hereby certify that JESSE MAYHO of free person of Color dark Complexion about twenty four years of age, five feet three inches high, has no Scar on face head or hands was born free as appears from the evidence of W Y MALLORY and is duly registered in my Office this 28th day of August 1843.

Register No. 477 E. R Turnbull CLK
Wm H E Merritt JP.

Brunswick County Court Augst term 1843
The above certificate was compared by the Court with the person of Said JESSE MAYHO and found to be correct.

E R Turnbull CLK

=====

Brunswick County to wit

I do hereby Certify that the bearer PETER MAYHO a free person of Color yellow Complexion about thirty five years of age, five feet eight & a half inches high has a Scar under his Chin, was born free as appears from a former Certificate, and is duly registered in my Office this 25 day of Sept. 1843.

Register No. 478 E R Turnbull CLK
Jos H Travis JP

Brunswick County Court Sept term 1843 (1843)
The above certificate was compared by the Court with the person of the said PETER MAYHO and found to be Correct.

Teste E R Turnbull CLK

=====

Brunswick County to wit

I do hereby Certify that the bearer hereof POLLY MAYHO a free person of Color, dark Complexion about forty five years of age, five feet three inches high, has no scar on face head or hands was born free as appears from the evidence of WM Y MALLORY and is duly registered in my Office this 25 Sept. 1843.

Register No. 479 E R Turnbull CLK
B B Wilkes JP

Brunswick County Court Sept term 1843
The above Certificate was Compared by the Court with the person of the said POLLY MAYHO & found to be Correct.

Teste E R Turnbull CLK

=====

Brunswick County to wit
I do hereby certify that the bearer hereof BILLY MAYHO a free person of Color, dark Complexion about twenty four years of age, five feet three ¼ Inches high has a scar on left thumb, was born free as appears from the evidence of WM Y MALLORY and is duly registered in my Office the 25th Sept 1843.

Register No. 480 E R Turnbull CLK
B B Wilkes
Brunswick County Court Sept term 1843
The above Certificate was compared by the Court with the person of the Said BILLY MAYHO and found to be Correct.
Teste E R Turnbull CLK

=====

Brunswick County to wit
I do hereby Certify that the bearer hereof SAMUEL MAYHO a free person of Color, dark Complexion about twenty one years of age five feet five Inches high has no Scar on face head or hands, was born free as appears from the evidence of WM Y MALLORY and is duly registered in my Office this 25 Sept 1843

Register No 481 E R Turnbull CLK
B B Wilkes JP
Brunswick County County (sic) Sept term 1843
The above Certificate was compared by the Court with the person of the said SAMUEL MAYHO & found to be correct.
E R Turnbull CLK

=====

Brunswick County to wit
I do hereby certify that the bearer hereof BENJAMIN MANNING a free person of Color dark Complexion, about thirty one years of age five feet ten inches high has one Scar on left Cheek was born free as appears from the evidence of BENJA D CHAPMAN and is duly registered in my Office this 27 day of Decr. 1841

Register No. 482 E R Turnbull DCLK
F W Green JP
Brunswick County Court Sept term 1843
The above certificate was Compared by the Court with the person of the said BENJA MANNING & found to be correct.
Teste E R Turnbull CLK

=====

Brunswick County to wit
I do hereby Certify that the bearer hereof HINSON MANNING a free person of Color dark Complexion about twenty five years of age, five feet Sevin inches high, has one Scar on thumb of left hand was born free as appears from the evidence of DRURY D NANNY and is duly registered in my Office this 25 Sept. 1843.

Register No. 483 E R Turnbull CLK
B B Wilkes
Brunswick County Court Sept term 1843
The above Certificate was compared by the Court with the person of said HINSON MANNING & found to be correct.
E R Turnbull CLK

=====

Brunswick County to wit
I do hereby certify that the bearer hereof LUCY MANNING a free person of Color, dark Complexion about twenty Seven years of age, five feet Seven Inches high has no Scar on face head or hands was born free as appears from the evidence of DRURY D NANNY and is duly registered in my Office this 25 Sept 1843.

Register No. 484 E R Turnbull CLK
B B Wilkes
Brunswick County Court Sept term 1843
The above certificate was compared by the Court with the person of the said LUCY MANNING & found to be correct.
Teste E R Turnbull CLK

=====

Brunswick County to wit
I do hereby certify that the bearer hereof FRANK ATKINS a free person of Color dark Complexion, about twenty six years of age, five feet ten & a half inches high has one Scar on fore finger, and back of left hand, was born free as appears from the evidence of B D CHAPMAN and is duly registered in my Office this 25 Sept 1843.

Register No. 485 E R Turnbull CLK
Jno P Atkinson JP
Brunswick County Court Sept term 1843
The above certificate was compared by the Court with the person of Said FRANK ATKINS and found to be Correct.
E R Turnbull CLK

=====

Brunswick County, to wit:

I do hereby certify that the bearer hereof FANNY EASTER a free person of color, dark complexion about twenty seven years of age, five feet eight inches high, has one Scar on her right wrist was born free as appears from the evidence of F. W GREEN and is duly registered in my office this 23rd day of Oct. 1843.

Register No. 486 E R Turnbull CLK
B B Wilkes JP

Brunswick County Court Oct term 1843

The above certificate was compared by the Court with the person of the said FANNY EASTER and found to be correct.

Teste E R Turnbull CLK

=====

Brunswick County to wit

I do hereby certify, that the bearer hereof ROBERTA MALONE a free person of color dark Complexion about twenty two years of age, five feet two inches high, has one scar on left hand, was born free as appears from the evidence of P H BUCKLEY and is duly registered in my office this 27 day of Nov. 1843.

Register No. 487 E R Turnbull
R H H Wallton

Brunswick County Court Nov. Term 1843

The above certificate was compared by the Court, with the person of the said ROBERTA MALONE & found to be correct.

Teste E R Turnbull CLK

=====

State of Virginia
Brunswick County to wit

I hereby certify that the bearer hereof JNO. OWEN a free person of Color dark Complexion, about 22 years of Age, 5 feet 10 inches high, has a Scar on right Side of Chin, one on back of left hand, and one on left wrist, was born free, as appears from the evidence of A MALLORY and is duly registered in my Office this 25th day of Mar. 1844.

Register No. 488 E R Turnbull Clerk
B B Wilkes JP

Brunswick County Court Mar term 1844

The above certificate was compared by the Court with the person of the Said OWEN & found to be correct.

Teste E R Turnbull CCC

=====

39   E R Turnbull CC

wick County Court Apl term 1844
ficate was compared, by the Court, with the person of
EASTER, and found to be correct.
Teste   E R Turnbull CC

nia

y to wit
eby Certify that the bearer hereof PEGGY STEWART a
Color yellow complexion about 22 years of age 5 feet
has no scar on face head or hands was born free as
e evidence of G W GREEN and is duly registered in my
day of Apl 1844.

0   E R Turnbull CC
JP
wick County Court Apl term 1844
ficate was Compared by the Court with the person of
STEWART and found to be correct.
Teste   E R Turnbull CC

nia

y to wit
eby Certify that the bearer hereof MARTHA STEWART a
Color yellow Complexion about 23 years of age 5 feet
has no Scar on face head or hands was born free as
e evidence of G. W. GREEN and is duly registered in my
Apl 1844.

1   E R Turnbull
JP
swick County Court Apl term 1844
ificate was compared by the Court with the person of the
& found to be correct.
Teste   E R Turnbull CC

Brunswick County to wit
I do hereby certify, that the bearer hereof MARY ATKINS a free person of Color, dark Complexion, about 21 years of age 4 feet 11 inches high has one scar on right wrist, was born free as appears from the evidence of R H H WALLTON and is duly registered in my Office this 28 August 1843.

Register No. 492 E R Turnbull CLK
Wm H E Merritt JP
Brunswick County Court August term 1844
The above certificate was compared by the Court with the person of the said MARY ATKINS & found to be correct.
Teste E R Turnbull CLK

=====

State of Virginia

Brunswick County to wit
I hereby certify, that the bearer hereof DAVID EDMUNDS free person of color Dark Complexion about 24 years of age, 5 feet 5 inches high, has one scar over each eye, one on back of right hand & one on left thumb was born free, as appears from a former Certificate and is duly registered in my Office this 24 day of June 1844.
Register No. 493 E R Turnbull Clerk
John P Atkinson JP
Brunswick County Court June term 1844
The above certificate was compared by the Court with the person of the said DAVID EDMUNDS & found to be correct.
Teste E R Turnbull Clerk

=====

State of Virginia

Brunswick County to wit
I hereby certify, that the bearer hereof WM D KENNEDY, a free person of Color dark Complexion about 38 years of age 5 feet 8½ inches high, has no scar on face head or hands, was born free as appears from a former certificate & is duly registered in my Office this 22 day of July 1844

Register No. 494 E R Turnbull CLK
Brunswick County Court July term 1844
The above certificate was compared by the Court with the person of the said WM D KENNEDY & found to be correct.
Teste E R Turnbull Clerk

=====

Brunswick County to wit
I do hereby certify that LUCY MERRITT a free person of Color dark complexion about thirty three years of age five feet nine inches high has a scar on the back of her left hand & one on her right Jaw, was born free as appears from the evidence of F W GREEN and is duly registered in my Office this 24 day of Feby 1840.

R H H Wallton　　　　　　　　　　　　Chas. Turnbull CC
Register No. 495
Brunswick County Court Feby term 1840
The above certificate was compared by the Court with the person of said LUCY MERRITT & found to be correct.
Teste　　E R Turnbull Clerk

=====

Brunswick County to wit
I do hereby certify, that the bearer hereof VIRGINIA MERRITT a free person of Color Dark Complexion about twenty three years of age, 5 feet 5½ inches high has two scars on the left wrist, was born free as appears from the evidence of F W GREEN and is duly registered in my office this 25 day of October 1841.

E B Tucker JP　　　　　　　　　　　　Charles Turnbull CC
Register No. 496
Brunswick County Court Oct. term 1841
The above certificate was compared by the Court with the person of the said VIRGINIA MERRITT & found to be correct.
Teste　　E R Turnbull Clerk

=====

State of Virginia

Brunswick County to wit
I hereby certify, that the bearer hereof RUFFIN JACKSON a free person of color yellow complexion about 21 years of age 5 feet 6½ inches high has No scar on face head or hands was born free as appears from the evidence of F W GREEN and is duly registered in my Office this 26 day of August 1844.

Register No. 497　　　　　　　　　　　　E R Turnbull Clerk
John Wyche JP
Brunswick County Court August term 1844
The above certificate was compared by the Court with the person of the said RUFFIN JACKSON & found to be correct.
Teste　　E R Turnbull CC

=====

State of Virginia

Brunswick County to wit
I hereby certify that the bearer hereof MANERVA MERRITT a free person of color dark complexion about 27 years of age 5 feet 9½ inches high, has one scar on right hand was born free, as appears from the evidence B. D. CHAPMAN and is duly registered in my Office this 23 day of Sept. 1844.

Register No. 498 E R Turnbull CLK
B. B. Wilkes
Brunswick County Court August term 1844
The above certificate was compared by the Court with the person of the said MANERVA MERRITT & found to be correct.
Teste E R Turnbull CLK

=====

State of Virginia

Brunswick County to wit
I hereby certify, that the bearer hereof WASHINGTON STEWART a free person of color yellow Complexion, about 21 years of age 6 feet ½ inches high, has no scar on face head or hands was born free, as appears from the evidence of B D CHAPMAN and is duly registered in my office, this 23 day of Sept 1844.

Register No. 499 E R Turnbull CLK
B B Wilkes
Brunswick County Court Sept term 1844
The above certificate was compared by the Court with the person of the said WASHINGTON STEWART & found to be correct.
Teste E R Turnbull

=====

Brunswick County to wit
I do hereby certify that the bearer hereof JANE EASTER a free person of color yellow complexion about twenty years of age 5 feet 1 inch ½ high has two small scars on the back of her right hand & one under her left eye on her Cheek, was born free as appears from the evidence of F W GREEN & is duly registered in my Office this 24 day of Feby 1840

R H H Wallton Chas. Turnbull CC
Register No. 500
Brunswick County Court Feby term 1840
The above certificate was compared by the Court with the person of the said JANE EASTER & found to be correct.
Teste E R Turnbull

=====

State of Virginia

Brunswick County to wit
I hereby certify that the bearer hereof SALLY EASTER a free person of color, dark Complexion about 25 years of age 5 feet 4 inches high has one scar on back of right hand one on middle finger and one on back of left hand was born free as appears from the evidence of B D CHAPMAN and is duly registered in my Office this 23 day of Sept 1844.

Register No. 501 E R Turnbull CLK
B B Wilkes
Brunswick County Court Sept term 1844
The above certificate was compared by the Court, with the person of the said SALLY EASTER & found to be correct.
Teste E R Turnbull CLK

=====

State of Virginia

Brunswick County to wit
I hereby certify, that the bearer hereof MIMA MALONE a free person of color yellow Complexion 18 years of age 5 feet 1 inch high, has no scar on face head or hands was born free, as appears from the evidence of WM H MITCHELL and is duly registered in my Office this 25 day of Nov 1844.

Register No. 502 E R Turnbull Clerk
Jno P Atkinston JP
Brunswick County Court Nov term 1844
The above certificate was compared by the Court with the person of the said MIMA MALONE & found to be correct.
Teste E R Turnbull Clerk

=====

State of Virginia

Brunswick County to wit
I hereby certify, that the bearer hereof DAVID EDMUNDS a free person of Color Dark Complexion about 24 years of age 5 feet 4 inches high, has one scar over each eye, one on left thumb, and one on back of left hand, was born free as appears from a former certificate and is duly registered in my Office this 24 day of Feby 1845.

Register No. 503 E R Turnbull ClK
John Wyche
Brunswick County Court Feby term 1845
The above Certificate was compared by the Court with the person of the said DAVID EDMUNDS and found to be correct.
Teste E R Turnbull CK

=====

State of Virginia

Brunswick County to wit

I hereby Certify, that the bearer hereof JACK DANIEL, a free person of Color yellow complexion, about 25 years of age 5 feet 8 inches high, has no scar on face head or hands, was born free as appears from the evidence of S C PEARSON and is duly registered in my office, this 24 Mar 1845.

Register No 504 E R Turnbull Clerk
R H H Walton

Brunswick County Court Mar term 1845
The above certificate was compared by the Court, with the person of the said JACK DANIEL & found to be correct.

E R Turnbull Clerk

=====

State of Virginia)
)
Brunswick County to wit)

I hereby certify, that the bearer hereof THOS W LEWIS a free person of color, yellow complexion, about 23 years of age 5 fee 6 inches high, has one mark or Scar near right eye was born free, a appears from the evidence of WM Y MALLORY and is duly registered in my Office this 28 day of Apl 1845.

Register No. 505 E R Turnbull Clerk
Jno Wyche

Brunswick County Court Apl term 1845
The above certificate was compared by the Court, with the person of the said THOS W LEWIS and found to be correct.

Teste E R Turnbull CLK

=====

Brunswick County to wit

I hereby certify that the bearer hereof URIAS ROBERTS a free person of colour Dark Complexion about 24 years of age five fee eight inches & ½ high has a scar under the right eye and one between the four finger & thumb of the right hand born free as appears from the evidence of STERLING C PEARSON & is duly registered in my Office this 24 Jany 1842.

Register No. 506 Chas Turnbull CBC
F W Green

Brunswick County Court Jany term 1842
The above certificate was compared by the Court with the person of the said URIAS ROBERTS & found to be correct.

Chas Turnbull CLK

=====

State of Virginia)
)
Brunswick County to wit)

I hereby certify, that the bearer hereof WM MERRITT a free person of Color Dark Complexion about 22 years of age 5 feet 8 inches high, has Several Scars on back of his hands and one on third finger of right hand was born free as appears from the evidence of GEO SHORT and is duly registered in my office this 25 day of Aug 1845.

Register No. 507 E R Turnbull ClK
Wm Meredith JP

Brunswick County Court Aug term 1845
The above certificate was compared by the Court with the person of the Said WM MERRITT and found to be correct.

Teste E R Turnbull CLK

=====

State of Virginia)
)
Brunswick County, to wit:)

I hereby certify that the bearer hereof FANNY EDMUNDS a free person of color dark complexion about twenty years of age, five feet, two inches high has one scar on forehead, was born free, as appears from the evidence of THOMAS KIRKLAND, and is duly registered in my office this 27th day of January 1845.

Register No. 508 E R Turnbull Clerk
R H H Wallton JP

Brunswick County Court March term 1845
The above certificate was compared by the Court with the person of the said FANNY EDMUNDS & found to be correct.

Teste E R Turnbull Clerk

=====

State of Virginia)
)
Brunswick County to wit)

I hereby certify that the bearer hereof BETSY GILLIS a free person of color, dark complexion, about 22 years of age 5 feet 7½ inches high, has four scars on back of right hand and one on left thumb, was born free as appears from the evidence of R H H WALLTON and is duly registered in my office this 23 Mar 1846.

Register No. 509 E R Turnbull CLK
E H H Blick

Brunswick County Court Mar term 1846
The above certificate was compared by the Court with the person of said BETSY GILLIS and found to be correct.

E R Turnbull CLK

=====

State of Virginia

Brunswick County to wit

I hereby certify, that the bearer hereof FORTUNE MERRITT a free person of color dark Complexion about 19 years of age 5 feet 7½ inches high has 2 scars on back of right hand & one on left hand, was born free, as appears from the evidence of R. H. H. WALLTON and is duly registered in my office this 23 Mar 1846.

Register No. 510 E R Turnbull CLK
E H H Blick

Brunswick County Court Mar term 1846

The above certificate was compared by the Court with the person of the said FORTUNE MERRITT & found to be correct.

E R Turnbull CLK

=====

State of Virginia

Brunswick County to wit

I hereby certify that JESSE GILLIS a free person of color Dark Complexion about 22 years of age, 5 feet 5 inches high, has no scar on face head or hands, was born free as appears from the evidence of R H H WALLTON, and is duly registered in my Office this 23 Mar 1846.

Register No. 511 E R Turnbull CLK
E H H Blick

Brunswick County Court Mar term 1846

The above certificate was compared by the Court, with the person of the said JESSE GILLIS, & found to be correct.

E R Turnbull CLK

=====

State of Virginia

Brunswick County to wit

I hereby certify, that the bearer hereof MARTHA GRAIN a free person of color yellow complexion about 23 years of age 5 feet 4 inches high has one scar on left thumb, was born free as appears from the evidence of PASCAL HICKS and is duly registered in my Office this 27 day of July 1846.

Register No. 512 E R Turnbull CLK
B B wilkes JP

Brunswick County Court July term 1846

The above certificate was compared by the Court with the person of the said MARTHA GRAIN & found to be correct.

E R Turnbull CLK

=====

State of Virginia

Brunswick County to wit
I hereby certify that the bearer hereof THOMAS W SMITH a free person of color yellow complexion about 22 years of age five feet eleven inches high has one scar on back of left hand was born free as appears from the evidence of PASCAL HICKS and is duly registered in my Office this 25 Aug 1845.

Register No. 513 E R Turnbull CLK
Wm Meredith JP
Brunswick County Court July 1846
The above certificate was compared by the Court with the person of the said THOS W SMITH & found to be correct.
E R Turnbull CLK

=====

State of Virginia

Brunswick County to wit
I hereby certify that the bearer hereof NANCY SMITH a free person of color yellow complexion about 21 years of age 5 feet 3 3/4 inches high has no scar on face head or hands, was born free as appears from the evidence of PASCAL HICKS and is duly registered in my Office this 27 day of July 1846.

Register No. 514 E R Turnbull CLK
B. B. Wilkes
Brunswick County Court July term 1846
The above certificate was compared by the Court, with the person of the said NANCY SMITH & found to be correct.
E R Turnbull CLK

=====

State of Virginia

Brunswick County to wit
I hereby certify that GODFRY OWEN a free person of color yellow Complexion about 21 years of age 5 feet 11 inches high, has one scar over the left eye and one on back of right hand was born free as appears from the evidence of ALEX MALLORY and is duly registered in my Office this 27 July 1846.
B. B Wilkes JP
Register No. 515 E R Turnbull CLK
The above certificate was compared by the Court with the person of the said GODFRY OWEN JR & found to be correct.
E R Turnbull CLK

=====

State of Virginia)
)
Brunswick County, to wit)

I hereby certify that the bearer hereof POLLY CHAVIS a free person of color, dark complexion, about forty years of age five feet three inches high, has no scar on face head or hands, was born free as appears from the evidence of E H H BLICK and is duly registered in my office, this 19th day of March 1847.

Register No. 516 E R Turnbull CLK
R H H Wallton JP

Brunswick County Court Mar term 1847

The above certificate was compared by the court with the person of the said POLLY CHAVIS & found to be correct.

E R Turnbull CLK

=====

State of Virginia)
)
Brunswick County, to wit:)

I hereby certify that the bearer hereof JOSEPH MAYHO a free person of color, dark complexion, about fifty years of age 5 feet 6 inches high, has no scar on face, head or hands, was born free as appears from the evidence of E H H BLICK and is duly registered in my Office this 19th day of March 1847.

Register No. 517 E R Turnbull CLK
R H H Wallton JP

Brunswick County Court Mar term 1847

The above certificate was compared by the Court with the person of said JOS. MAYHO & found to be correct.

Teste E R Turnbull CLK

=====

State of Virginia

Brunswick County to wit

I hereby certify, that the bearer hereof MATILDA MAYHO a free person of color, dark complexion, about nine years of age, 5 feet 2½ inches high has a scar near left corner of mouth was born free as appears from the evidence of E H BLICK and is duly registered in my office this 19th day of March 1847.

Register No. 518 E R Turnbull CLK
R H H Wallton JP

Brunswick County Court Mar term 1847

The above certificate was compared by the Court with the person of the said MATILDA MAYHO & found to be correct.

Teste E R Turnbull CLK

=====

State of Virginia)
)
Brunswick County, to wit:)

I hereby certify, that the bearer hereof KITTY CHAVIS a free person of color, yellow complexion about twenty years of age, four feet 10 3/4 inches high, has no scar on face head or hands was born free as appears from the evidence of E H BLICK and is duly registered in my office this 19th day of March 1847

Register No. 519 E R Turnbull CLK
R H H Wallton JP

Brunswick County Court Mar term 1847
The above certificate was compared by the court with the person of said KITTY CHAVIS & found to be correct.

Teste E R Turnbull CLK

=====

State of Virginia)
)
Brunswick County to wit)

I hereby certify, that the bearer hereof MARTHA MC KENNY a free person of color, yellow Complexion, about 23 years of age 5 feet 4½ inches high, has one scar on middle of forehead, was born free as appears from the evidence of RO. L. COLEMAN and is duly registered in my office this 25 Oct 1847.

Register No. 520 E R Turnbull CLK
J B Mallory JP

Brunswick County Court Oct term 1847
The above certificate, was compared by the Court, with the person of the said MARTHA MC KINNY & found to be correct.

E R Turnbull CLK

=====

State of Virginia)
)
Brunswick County)

I hereby certify, that the bearer hereof JAMES H A MALONE a free person of color Dark Complexion 31 years of age 5 feet 7¼ inches high has one scar on upper part of forehead, & one on right cheek was born free as appears from the evidence of DAVID J JOHNSON & is duly registered in my office this 27th day of Dec. 1847.

Register No. 521 E R Turnbull CLK
B B wilkes J. P.

Brunswick County Court Dec. term 1847
The above certificate was compared by the Court with the person of the said JAS H A MALONE & found to be correct.

E R Turnbull CLK

=====

State of Virginia)
)
Brunswick County)

I hereby certify that the bearer hereof, WM TUCKER a free person of color, yellow complexion, about 24 years of age 6 feet high, has no scars on face head or hands, was emancipated by the wil of HEARTWELL TUCKER and is duly registered in my office this 28th Feby. 1848.

Register No. 522 E R Turnbull CLK
Wm Meredith J. P.

Brunswick County Court Feby term 1848
The above certificate was compared by the Court with the person of the said WM TUCKER & found to be correct.

E R Turnbull CLK

=====

State of Virginia

Brunswick County to wit

I hereby certify that the bearer hereof WM LATIMORE a free person of color dark Complexion, about 26 years of age, five feet nine and a half inches high, has no scar on face head or hands, was emancipated by the will of JOHN LATIMORE and is duly registered in my Office, this 28 day of February 1848.

Register No. 523 E R Turnbull CLK
Wm Meredith J. P.

Brunswick County Court Febry. term 1848
The above certificate was compared by the Court, with the person of the said WILLIAM LATIMORE & found to be correct.

E R Turnbull CLK

=====

State of Virginia)
)
Brunswick County)

I hereby certify, that the bearer hereof NAT PELHAM a free person of color, dark complexion about 22 years of age 5 feet 5 3/4 inches high, has one scar in the middle of forehead one between the eyes and one on the fourth finger of right hand was born free, as appears from the evidence of ROBT K THACKER and is duly registered in my Office this 28 day of Dec. 1846

Register No. 524 E R Turnbull CLK
John P Atkinson

Brunswick County Court Dec. term 1846
The above certificate was compared by the Court with the person of said NAT PELHAM & found to be correct.

E R Turnbull CLK

=====

State of Virginia)
)
Brunswick County to wit)

I hereby certify, that the bearer hereof THOMAS STEWART a free person of color yellow complexion, about 55 years of age 5 feet 5 inches high, has a scar just above the cheek bone near the left eye, was Emancipated as appears from a former certificate, and is duly registered in my office, this 26th day of June 1848.

Register No. 525 E R Turnbull CLK
R H H Wallton J. P.

Brunswick County Court July term 1848
The above certificate was compared by the Court, with the person of the said THOMAS STEWART, & found to be correct.

E R Turnbull CLK

=====

State of Virginia)
)
Brunswick County to wit)

I hereby certify that the bearer hereof FREDK GRAVES a free person of Color, dark complexion, about 30 years of age, 5 feet 6 inches high, has one scar on left side of forehead, one on right side of throat and one on back of left hand near the thumb, was born free, as appears from the evidence of D J CLAIBORNE JR and is duly registered in my Office, this 24th day of July 1848.

Register No. 526 E R Turnbull CLK
R H H Wallton

Brunswick County Court July term 1848
The above certificate was compared by the Court, with the person of the said FREDK GRAVES & found to be correct.

E R Turnbull CLK

=====

State of Virginia)
)
Brunswick County to wit)

I hereby certify that the bearer hereof RODOLPHUS W LEWIS a free person of Color dark complexion 21 years of age 5 feet 10 3/4 inches high has a scar on left fore finger, one on left eye brow, and one at corner of right eye was born free, as appears from the evidence of JAMES B MALLORY and is duly registered in my office this 22nd day of July 1848.

Register No. 527 E R Turnbull CLK
R. H. H. Wallton

Brunswick County Court July term 1848
The above certificate was compared by the Court with the person of the said RODOLPHUS LEWIS and found to be correct.

E R Turnbull CLK

=====

State of Virginia)
)
Brunswick County to wit)

I hereby certify that the bearer hereof DANL MERRITT a free person of color, dark complexion 21 years of age 5 feet 2½ inches high has two Scars on left wrist, was born free, as appears from the evidence of J. H. JOHNSON JR and is duly registered in my office this twenty fourth day of July one thousand eight hundred and forty eight.

Register No. 528 E R Turnbull CLK
R H H Wallton JP

Brunswick County Court July term 1848
The above certificate, was compared by the Court with the person of the said DAN'L MERRITT & found to be correct.

E R Turnbull CLK

=====

State of Virginia)
)
Brunswick to wit)

I hereby certify that, the bearer hereof BETSY POMPY a free person of color, yellow complexion about 39 years of age 5 feet 6 inches high, has one scar on middle finger of left hand was born free, as appears from the evidence of R. H. H. WALLTON and is duly registered in my office, this 23rd Apl 1849.

Register No. 529 E R Turnbull CLK
Wmsson Kelly J. P.

Brunswick County Court Apl term 1849
The above certificate was compared by the Court with the person of the said BETSY POMPY & found to be correct.

E R Turnbull CLK

=====

State of Virginia)
)
Brunswick County to wit)

I hereby certify that the bearer hereof LOUISA CAIN a free person of color, yellow complexion about 25 years of age 5 feet 8 inches high, has a small scar over the right eye and one on back of left hand, was born free, as appears from the evidence of WMSSON KELLY and is duly registered in my office this 27th day of March 1849

Register No. 530 E R Turnbull CLK
J. A. Riddick

Brunswick County Court May term 1849
The above certificate was compared by the Court, with the person of the said LOUISA CAIN & found to be correct.

E R Turnbull CLK

=====

State of Virginia)
)
Brunswick County to wit)

I hereby certify that the bearer hereof WM H STEWARD a free person of Color yellow Complexion, 21 years of age 6 feet 3/4 inches high, has a scar on left thumb & one near left wrist, was born free, as appears from the evidence of R. T. STONE, and is duly registered in my office, this 23rd day of Oct. 1848.

Register No. 531 E R Turnbull CLK
J. A. Riddick

Brunswick County Court May term 1849
The above certificate, was compared by the Court, with the person of the said WM H. STEWARD, and found to be correct.

E R Turnbull CLK

=====

State of Virginia

Brunswick County to wit

I hereby certify, that the bearer hereof RUFFIN EASTER, a free person of Color, Dark complexion, about 21 years of age, 5 feet 11½ inches high, has one scar over four finger of right hand, one on knuckle of middle finger of right hand & one on back of right hand was born free, as appears from the evidence of WMSSON KELLY, and is duly registered, in my Office, this 28th day of May 1849.

Register No. 532 E R Turnbull CLK
B. B. Wilkes J. P.

Brunswick County Court May term 1849
The above certificate, was compared by the Court, with the person of the said RUFFIN EASTER, & found to be correct.

E R Turnbull CLK

=====

State of Virginia

Brunswick County to wit

I hereby certify that the bearer hereof ROBT EASTER a free person of Color Dark complexion about 24 years of age 5 feet 7½ inches high, has one scar in palm of the left hand near the wrist, was born free as appears from the evidence of W. J. HOBBS and is duly registered in my Office this 23rd July 1849.

Register No. 533 E R Turnbull CLK
R. H. H. Wallton J. P.

Brunswick County Court July term 1849
The above certificate was comapred by the Court with the person of the said ROBT. EASTER & found to be correct.

E R Turnbull CLK

=====

State of Virginia

Brunswick County to wit
I hereby certify, that the bearer hereof MARGARET EASTER a free person of Color Dark Complexion, about 19 years of age, 5 feet 3 inches high, has no scar on face head or hands, was born free as appears from the evidence of WMSSON KELLY & is duly registered in my Office this 23rd July 1849.

Register No. 534 E R Turnbull CLK
R. H. H. Wallton J. P.
Brunswick County Court July term 1849
The above certificate, was compared by the Court, with the person of the said MARGARET EASTER & found to be correct.
E R Turnbull CLK

=====

State of Virginia

Brunswick County to wit
I hereby certify, that the bearer hereof MARY EASTER a free person of Color yellow complexion about 19 years of age 5 feet 6 inches high, has one scar on right & one on left cheek. one on knuckle of fourth finger of right hand & one on knuckle of middle finger of left hand was born free, as appears from the evidence of R. H. H. WALLTON and is duly registered in my Office, this 23d day of July 1849.
Register No. 535 E R Turnbull CLK
Luke J. Palmer J. P.
Brunswick County Court July term 1849
The above certifcate was compared by the Court, with the person of the said MARY EASTER & found to be correct.
E R Turnbull CLK

=====

State of Virginia

Brunswick County to wit
I hereby certify, that the bearer hereof GOVAN EASTER a free person of Color yellow complexion, about 21 years of age 5 feet 8 inches high, has one scar on middle finger of left hand, one on middle finger of right hand & one on little finger of right hand, was born free, as appears from the evidence of W. J. HOBBS and is duly registered in my Office this 23d July 1849.

Register No. 536 E R Turnbull CLK
R. H. H. Wallton J. P.
Brunswick County Court July term 1849
The above certificate, was compared by the Court with the person of the said, GOVAN EASTER & found to be correct.
E R Turnbull CLK

=====

State of Virginia

Brunswick County to wit
I hereby certify, that the bearer hereof SUSAN CHAPMAN a free person of color dark Complexion, about 33 years of age 5 feet 1 3/4 inches high, has one Scar on throat, was born free, as appears from a former certificate, & is duly registered in my Office, this 23d day of July 1849.

Register No. 537 E R Turnbull CLK
R. H. H. Wallton J. P.
Brunswick County Court July term 1849
The above certificate, was compared by the Court, with the person of the said SUSAN CHAPMAN & found to be correct.
E R Turnbull CLK

=====

State of Virginia

Brunswick County to wit
I hereby certify that the bearer hereof LUCINDA STEWART a free person of color, yellow Complexion, about 20 years of age, 5 feet 5½ inches high, has one scar on right side of neck, was born free as appears from the evidence of W. J. HOBBS, and is duly registered in my Office this 23d day of July 1849.

Register No. 538 E R Turnbull CLK
R. H. H. Wallton J. P.
Brunswick County Court July term 1849
The above certificate, was compared by the Court with the person of the said LUCINDA STEWART & found to be correct.
E R Turnbull CLK

=====

State of Virginia)
)
Brunswick County, to wit)
I hereby certify, that the bearer hereof HICKS GRAIN a free person of color, dark complexion, about forty years of age, five feet five inches high, has one scar on left cheek, and one on fourth finger of left hand was born free as appears from a former certificate and is duly registered in my office, this 23 day of July 1849.

Register No. 539 E R Turnbull CLK
R. H. H. Wallton JP
Brunswick County Court July term 1849
The above certificate was compared by the Court with the person of said HICKS GRAIN & found to be correct.
Teste E R Turnbull CLK

=====

State of Virginia)
)
Brunswick County, to wit)

I hereby Certify, that the bearer hereof FANNY MERRITT a free person of color. dark complexion about fortv years of age; 5 feet 3 inches high has one scar over left eye, was born free as appears from a former certificate, and is duly registered in my office this 23d July 1849.

Register No. 540 E R Turnbull ClK
R H H Wallton JP

Brunswick County Court July term 1849
The above certificate was compared by the Court with the person of said FANNY MERRITT & found to be correct.

Teste E R Turnbull CLK

=====

State of Virginia)
)
Brunswick County, to wit)

I hereby certify that the bearer hereof DAVID EDMUNDS a free person of color, dark complexion about 27 years of age; 5 feet 4½ Inches high, has one scar over each eye, one on left thumb & one on back of right hand, was born free, as appears from a former certificate and is duly registered in my office this 25th day of Sept 1848.

Register No. 541 E R Turnbull CLK
B B Wilkes

Brunswick County Court June term 1849
The above certificate was compared by the Court with the person of said DAVID EDMUNDS & found to be correct.

Teste E R Turnbull CLK

=====

State of Virginia)
)
Brunswick County)

I hereby certify that the bearer hereof JOHN ROBERTS a free person of color, yellow Complexion, about 22 years of age 5 feet 7 inches high has one scar on back of left hand was born free, as appears from the evidence of W. J. HOBBS & is duly registered in my Office this 23d day of July 1849.

Register No. 542 E R Turnbull CLK
R. H. H. Wallton J. P.

Brunswick County Court July term 1849
The above certificate was compared by the Court with the person of the said JOHN ROBERTS & found correct.

E R Turnbull CLK

=====

State of Virginia)
)
Brunswick County, to wit:)

I hereby certify that the bearer hereof MARY JANE EASTER a free person of color, dark complexion about nineteen years of age, 4 feet 11 inches high has 2 scars on forehead, one on left wrist, one on back right hand & one on back of left hand was born free, as appears from the evidence of W J HOBBS and is duly registered in my office this 23 day of July 1849.

Register No. 543 E R Turnbull CLK
R H H Wallton JP

Brunswick County Court July term 1849
The above certificate was compared by the Court with the person of said EASTER & found to be correct.

Teste E R Turnbull CLK

=====

State of Virginia)
)
Brunswick County to wit)

I hereby certify that the bearer hereof JACK MANNING a free person of color yellow complexion, about 22 years of age 5 feet 5 inches high has no scar on face head or hands was born free as appears from the evidence of JAMES RUFFIN SEWARD and is duly registered in my office this 25 Mar 1850.

Register No 544 E R Turnbull CLK
R H H Wallton

Brunswick County Ct. Mar term 1850
The above certificate was compared by the Court with the person of the said JACK MANNING & found to be correct.

E R Turnbull CLK

=====

State of Virginia)
)
Brunswick County, to wit)

I hereby certify, that the bearer hereof ROBERTA MOODY a free person of color, yellow complexion about thirty four years of age five feet four inches high, has a scar on back of right hand was born free as appears from a former certificate and is duly registered in my office this 25th day of March 1850.

Register No. 545 E R Turnbull CLK
R H H Wallton JP

Brunswick County Court March term 1850
The above certificate was compared by the Court with the person of said MOODY & found to be correct.

Teste E R Turnbull CLK

=====

State of Virginia)
)
Brunswick County, to wit)

I hereby certify that the bearer hereof SALLIE DANIEL a free person of color yellow complexion, about 26 years of age; five feet 4½ inches high, has one scar on right jaw was born free, as appears from the evidence of W. J. HOBBS and is duly registered in my office this 23 day of July 1849.

Register No. 546 E R Turnbull CLK
R H H Wallton JP

Brunswick County Court July term 1849
The above certificate was compared by the Court with the person of the said SALLY DANIEL & found to be correct.
Teste E R Turnbull Clerk

=====

State of Virginia)
)
Brunswick County, to wit)

I hereby certify that the bearer hereof MARTHA ANN SMITH a free person of color, yellow complexion, about twenty four years of age, four feet 7½ Inches high, has one scar under left jaw, was born free as appears from the evidence of STERLING C PEARSON and is duly registered in my office this 27th day of May 1850.

Register No. 547 E R Turnbull Clerk
R H H Wallton JP

Brunswick County Court May term 1850
The above certificate was compared by the Court with the person of said MARTHA ANN SMITH and found to be correct.
E R Turnbull Clerk

=====

State of Virginia)
)
Brunswick County, to wit)

I hereby certify, that the bearer hereof CLAIBORNE DANIEL a free person of color dark complexion about twenty three years of age, 5 feet 8½ Inches high has one scar in middle of forehead was born free as appears from the evidence of R H H WALLTON and is duly registered in my office this 27th May 1850.

Register No. 548 E R Turnbull Clerk
R H H Wallton JP

Brunswick County Court May term 1850
The above certificate was compared by the Court with the person of said DANIEL & found to be correct.
Teste E R Turnbull CLK

=====

State of Virginia)
)
Brunswick County, to wit;)

I hereby certify, that the bearer hereof NANCY ROBERTS a free person of color, dark complexion, about thirty years of age 5 feet 2¼ inches high, has one scar between finger & thumb of left hand was born free as appears from the evidence of R H H WALLTON, and is duly registered in my Office this 27 May 1850.

Register No. 549 E R Turnbull CLK
R H H Wallton JP

Brunswick County Court May term 1850
The above certificate was compared by the Court with the person of said ROBERTS & found to be correct.

Teste E R Turnbull CLK

=====

State of Virginia)
)
Brunswick County)

I hereby certify that the bearer hereof MIKE ADKINS a free person of Color dark complexion, about 22 years of age 6 feet ½ inch high, has one scar under right eye brow was born free as appears from the evidence of R H H WALLTON & is duly registered in my Office this 23 day of July 1849.

Register No. 550 E R Turnbull CLK
Luke J. Palmer JP

Brunswick County Court July term 1849
The above certificate, was compared by the Court, and found to be correct.

E R Turnbull CLK

=====

State of Virginia)
)
Brunswick County, to wit:)

I hereby certify, that the bearer hereof NANCY EASTER, a free person of color, dark complexion, about twenty two years of age, five feet seven inches high, has one scar on back of right hand, was born free as appears from the evidence of W. J. HOBBS and is duly registered in my office this 23d day of July 1849.

Register No. 551 E R Turnbull CLK
R H H Wallton JP

Brunswick County Court July term 1849
The above certificate was compared by the Court with the person of said EASTER & found to be correct.

E R Turnbull Clerk

=====

END of BOOK TWO

APPENDIX A

FREE BLACK
Brunswick County, Virginia, Federal Census 1810
M252 Roll # 66

Head of Household	Total	Head of Household	Total
		Inhabitants of Free Town	
Samuel Batten	1	Adam Abram	3
Pleasant Bugg	5	Arthur Allen	1
Betty Crook	2	Peter Bolling	1
Robert Crook	4	Daniel Cain	4
James Dabney	1	Peter Cain	8
Benjamin Edmunds	1	Henry Cain	1
Jack Hill	4	Welshire Easter	8
Fanny Hicks	6	Peter Faggan	1
James Jones	8	Edward James	6
James Jones	6	Robt James	3
Moses Jones	1	Charles Merritt	10
Samuel Jones	11	James Merritt	6
Robert Jones	1	John Mason	1
Abednigo Jones	3	Aaron Newsom	4
Earius Jones	4	Wm Pompey	1
Anthony Jones	1	Toyall (?) Porter	1
Topsail Jones	8	Abraham Robins	1
Sterling Lawrence	4	Adam Robins	1
Frederick Meredith	10	Wm Stewart	10
Toby Merritt	3	Dempsey Stewart	4
__illy Mathews	5	Roger Turnable	1
Thos Mathews	1	Joseph Ward	2
Luke Matthews	3	Mary Pompey	3
Dilcy Moss	3	Becky Pompey	3
Dick Merritt	1	Molly Roberts	5
Nathaniel Owen	1	Frank Atkins	1
Pompy Pelham	1	Gilvy Soward	2
Betty Pariss	5	Patience Harrison	6
__aris Stith	1		
John Walker	8		
Cupid Walker	3		
Peggy Walker	4		
Dick (?) Wilson	1		

APPENDIX B

FREE BLACK
BRUNSWICK COUNTY, VIRGINIA, FEDERAL CENSUS 1820
M33 ROLL # 134

Head of Family	SEX	Under 14	14-26	26-45	45 & up
p. 594 Pleasant Burg	M	1			2
	F	2	1		1
Robert Butler	M				1
	F				
p. 598 Billy Crook	M		2		
	F				
Wm Coleman	M				1
	F				
p. 600 Betty Crook	M				
	F		1		1
p. 604 Sam Freeman	M	1	2		
	F	5		1	
p. 606 Berry Hill	M		1		
	F				
p. 608 Jack Hill	M				1
	F				
Lewis Hicks	M				1
	F				
p. 610 Robert Hill	M				2
	F				
Sally Harrison	M	2	1		1
	F				1
Fanny Hicks	M	1			1
	F	1	1	3	1
p. 612 Abednigo Jones	M	3			1
	F	2			1
Ned Jones	M	4			1
	F				1
Sam M. Jones	M	4	2	1	
	F				1
Charles Jones	M	1		1	
	F		1		
Bob Jones	M	1		1	
	F		1		1
Godfrey Jones	M			1	
	F				
Enos Jones	M	4		4	1
	F	4	4	1	
Maria Jones	M	1			
	F	2	2	1	1
Phoebe Jones	M				
	F		2		1
Robert Jones	M			1	
	F				

Head of Family	SEX	Under 14	14-26	26-45	45 & up
p. 616 Edward L. Lewis	M		1		
	F				
Benjamin Lewis	M		1		
	F				
Daniel Lewis	M			1	
	F				1
p. 618 Frank Lawrence	M		1		
	F				
Jerry Lewis	M			2	
	F				
p. 620 John Mason	M			1	
	F				
Allen Moore	M			1	
	F				
Edmund Matthews	M			1	
	F	1	1	1	
Dick Merritt	M		1		
	F	5	1	1	1
Luke Matthews	M	4	2	1	
	F	2	1		
Nathaniel Moss	M	1	1	1	1
	F		1	1	
p. 624 Robert Owen	M	1		4	2
	F		2	1	
p. 626 Baker Parham	M			1	
	F				
p. 628 Frederick Rivers	M	1	1		1
	F	6	1	1	
Jack Roberts	M			1	
	F				
p. 630 Olive Scott	M				
	F	3	1		1
p. 636 John B. Thompson	M			1	
	F				
p. 638 Cupid Walker	M			21	1
	F				1
Moses Walker	M	1	2		
	F				
Arthur Walker	M			1	
	F				1
p. 640 Ned Walker	M		2	1	1
	F	1	2	3	1
Solomon Walker	M	2	1		1
	F	1	2		1
Mingo Walker	M			1	1
	F			2	2
Lud Walker	M		2	1	1
	F		2	1	

Head of Family	SEX	Under 14	14-26	26-45	45 & up
p. 642 Arthur Allen	M			1	
	F				
Adam Abrams	M	1	1	1	
	F			1	
Allen Atkins	M	2		1	2
	F	1	2	1	
Jeffrey Atkins	M				1
	F				
Mike Atkins	M			1	
	F				
p. 646 Godfrey Brown	M	1	5		1
	F	2	2	1	1
Peter Cain	M		1		
	F				
p. 646 Andrew Cain	M	2		1	
	F	1	1		
James Cain	M	1		1	
	F		1		
Anthony Cain	M	1		1	1
	F				
Daniel Cain	M				1
	F				
Richd Cain	M		1	1	
	F		2	1	
p. 648 Biddy Cousins	M	1			
	F		1	1	
Charles Chavis	M			1	
	F				
Lucy Chapman	M	1			
	F	3	1		1
Phillis Cain	M	2	1		
	F	1			1
p. 650 Isaac Edmunds	M			1	
	F				
Richd Evins	M	3			1
	F	2	1		
Enos Easter	M			1	
	F				
Wellshire Easter	M	2	3		1
	F	4	2	1	1
Jarrott Easter	M		1	1	
	F			1	
Brister Easter	M			1	
	F				
Dempsey Easter	M	2	1	1	1
	F	1		1	

Page	Name	Sex				
p. 652	Moses Grain	M	1		1	
		F	2	1	1	
	Matt Grain	M	3		1	
		F	2	2	1	
	Billy Grain	M		1		
		F				
	Thomas Graves	M			1	
		F	1	1		
	Sally Grain	M			1	
		F	3		1	
p. 656	Edward Hightower	M	4	2	1	1
		F	3	1	1	
	Isaac Hill	M		1		
		F				
	John Harris	M			1	
		F				
	Wm Herculas	M	3		1	
		F	2		1	
p. 658	Robin James	M	3		1	
		F			1	
	Ned James	M	1	1	1	
		F	2	1	1	
	Jensy Jones	M		1		
		F		1		
p. 660	Joseph Lewis	M			1	
		F				
p. 664	Stephen Malone	M	2		1	
		F	1	1		
	James Merritt	M	3	2	1	
		F	3		1	
	Charles Merritt	M	1	1	1	
		F	6	1	1	1
	Aaron Newsom	M	1		1	
		F	3	1		1
p. 666	Peggy Pompy	M	1			
		F	4	1	1	
	John Pellam	M	3	1	1	
		F	1		1	
p. 668	Lewis Roberts	M	6		1	1
		F	1	2	1	
	Abram Roberts	M	4	1	1	
		F	5			1
	Roger Roberts	M		1		
		F				

		SEX	Und	14	26	45
)	Dempsey Stewart	M				1
		F				1
	Wm Stewart	M	2	1		1
		F	1	1	2	1
	John Stewart	M	3		1	1
		F			1	
	Wm B. Stewart	M			1	
		F				
	Julius Stewart	M		1		
		F				
	Anthony Smith	M	3		1	
		F	2		1	
2	Thomas Valentine	M	1		1	
		F		1		
	Charles Valentine	M				1
		F				
3	Fanny Woodliff	M	3			
		F	1		1	
	Betsy Woodliff	M	5			
		F	1		2	1
	Robert Woodliff	M			1	
		F				

APPENDIX C

FREE BLACK
BRUNSWICK COUNTY, VIRGINIA, FEDERAL CENSUS 1830
M19 ROLL # 195

	Head of Family	SEX	Under 10	10-24	24-36	36-55	55-100	Over 100
p. 237	Atkins, Jeff	M	3		2		1	
		F		2	2			
	Atkins, Mike	M	4			1		
		F	2	2				
p. 238	Comitchell, Wm	M		1	1			
		F						
	Cain, Andrew	M		1		1		
		F		2		1		
	Cain, Richard	M	3	1	1	1		
		F	2	2	2	1		
	Cain, James	M	3	3	1		1	
		F	1	1			1	
	Cain, Polly	M	4					
		F			1			
p. 239	Douglas, Richd	M		1				
		F						
	Daniel, Moses	M				1		
		F	1	2		1		
p. 240	Easter, Dempsey	M	1			1		
		F	1		1			
	Easter, Wilcher	M	2				1	
		F			3			
	Gower, Frank	M	2		1		1	
		F		1				
	Gillis, Wm	M	3	3			1	
		F	1	2		1	1	
p. 241	Grain, Mat	M	1	2	1		1	
		F	1	2			1	
	Hunt, Fanny	M	1					
		F	1		1			
p. 242	Jones, Mary	M						
		F	1			1		
p. 243	Jones, Benj.	M					1	
		F					1	
p. 244	Merritt, Charles	M	2	1	1	1		
		F	3	3	3	1		
p. 245	Merritt, James	M	3	3		1		
		F	2	1	2	1		
	Main, Berry	M			1			
		F	3	1	1			
	Mitchell, Tillar	M	3		1			
		F		1				
	Mason, Wm	M	1					
		F		1				

Head of Family	SEX	Under 10	10-24	24-36	36-55	55-100	Over 100
p. 246 Owen, Green	M		1				
	F	2	1				
Owen, Fanny	M		1				
	F	3			1		
p. 247 Pelham, John	M		3		1		
	F	1	1				
Pompy, Turner	M		1				
	F	1	1			1	
p. 247 Pryor, Ned	M	1	2		1		
	F	2	3	1	1		
p. 248 Seward, Nancy	M	2	1				
	F		1		1	1	
Seward, Anna	M	2			1		
	F	3	1	1		1	
p. 249 Stewart, Dempsey	M		3			1	
	F					1	
Stewart, John	M		3	3	1		
	F	2	1	1			
Stewart, Wm	M	2	2	1		1	
	F	1	1		1		
Stewart, Littleton	M	3	1				
	F		1				
Smith, Berry	M			1			
	F	2		1			
p. 251 Woodley, Violet	M	2	2				
	F				1		
Woodley, Fanny	M	2	3	1			
	F	2	1		1		
p. 252 Atkins, Mike Jr (?)	M	1	1	1			
	F	1	2		1	1	
Atkins, Sally	M	2	2				
	F		2	1			
p. 253 Roberts, Liddy	M	1	2				
	F	2		1	1		
Roberts, Austen	M	2	2		1		
	F	1	1		1		
p. 259 Grain, Joseph	M	2	2	1			
	F	4	4	2	1		
p. 260 Hicks, Fanny	M		1	2			
	F	1	1	1	1		
Hill, Jack	M					1	
	F					1	
p. 262 Jones, Mary	M		1	1	1	1	
	F	1	2	1	1	1	
p. 264 Lewis, Edw.	M	3			2		
	F	1		3			

Head of Family	SEX	Under 10	10–24	24–36	36–55	55–100	Over 100
p. 265 Moss, Nat	M	1	1	2	1		
	F			1		1	
Malone, Patty	M	1	1			1	
	F	2	3		1		
p. 267 Pompy, Cressy	M	1					
	F	2		1			
p. 271 Thomas, Thomas B.	M	1	2		1		
	F	1		2		1	
p. 272 Valentine, James	M				1		
	F	1		1			

APPENDIX D

FREE BLACK
BRUNSWICK COUNTY, VIRGINIA, FEDERAL CENSUS 1840
M704 ROLL # 550

Head of Family	SEX	Under 10	10-24	24-36	36-55	55-100	Over 100
Sally Walton	M	2	1	2			
	F	5	1	1			
Bob Cain	M	1	1				
	F	4	1	2			
Jane Mise	M	1	1			1	
	F	1	2	1		1	
Travis Pelham	M	1	1				
	F		1				
Wm Merritt	M	1	2	1			
	F	1					
Jonas Moody	M	2	1		1		
	F	1		1			
Polly Cain	M	3					
	F	4	3	2			
John Stewart	M	2	1		1		
	F	2	4	1	1		
Austin Robbins	M	2	2			1	
	F		1	1		1	
Littleton Stewart	M	1	2		1		
	F	1		1			
Berry Smith	M	4			1		
	F		2		1		
R Stegall	M	1		1			
	F			1			
John Cain	M			1			
	F			1			
Patsey Valentine	M	1	2	1			
	F	1	3				
Parker Valentine	M	1	1				
	F	1					
Wm Valentine	M	1	1			1	
	F	1	1				
Bob Malone	M	1		1			
	F	1	1				
Gid Goldsbury	M	2	1	2	1		
	F	1	1		1		
Edward Malone	M	2	1	2	2	1	
	F	2	2	1	1		
Amos Butcher	M				1		
	F						
Henry Tatum	M	2	3	1	1		
	F	1	2	1			
Benj. Graves	M	5	4	2	1	1	
	F	2	3	4	1	1	

lly Merritt	F	1	1	2	1		
ses Walker	M				1		
	F						
y Coleman	M	2					
	F	1	1	1			
ngo Walker	M			2	1		
	F		1				
ram Roberts	M			2	4		
	F						
nnah Stith	M			2	4		
	F		1		1		
cob Walker	M				1		
	F						
rry Harrison	M	1	2	1	1		
	F	2	1	1			
b Butler	M			1			
	F						
wis Hicks	M				1		
	F						
rtha Malone	M	1					
	F	1	2		2		
nny Coleman	M						
	F		2	1			
lly Walker	M						
	F			3			
dfrey Jonas	M		1		1		
	F		1	1			
ter Mayho	M		1	1	1		
	F	1	2	1			
arles Mallory	M	2	2	1	1	1	
	F	2	1	3	2		
fred Cain	M			1			
	F						
ll Coleman	M			1			
	F						
Gallamore	M				1		
	F						
vid Merritt	M				1		
	F						
sse Mayho	M				1		
	F						
anbery Wright	M				1		
	F						
cob Merritt	M	2		1	1		
	F	1	1		1		
dfrey Owen	M	2	1	2			
	F	1	1	1			

Clerks of the Court

erbert Hill	1803-1816
Turnbull	1817-1839
arles Turnbull	1840-1843
R Turnbull	1843-1850

Justices of the Peace

1823
C. Cordle
Gray F. Dunn
James Rice
John B. Rice
James Wyche
John Wyche

1824
C. Cordle
J. B. Mallory
Nathaniel Mason
A. Powell
James Rice
Wm. (?) Rice

1825
John C. Chapman
Richard Fletcher
Daniel Hicks
Nathaniel E. Malry
James Rice
John Wyche

1826
F. W. Green
J. B. Mallory
James Rice
Edward C. Smith
John Tucker
John Wyche

1827
Wm Gholson
F. W. Green
J. B. Mallory
James Rice
John Wyche

1828
Benj. D. Chapman
F. W. Green
Daniel Hicks
James Rice
Isham Trotter
Burwell B. Wilkes
Wm. H. Worthington
John Wyche

1829
F. W. Green
Nathaniel E. Malry
R. F. Pritchett
James Rice
John Wyche

1830
J. B. Mallory
John Manning
Edward C. Smith
John Wyche

1831
Benj. D. Chapman
F. W. Green
Creed Haskins
John Manning
A. Powell
Edward C. Smith
Isham Trotter
Burwell B. Wilkes
John Wyche

1832
F. W. Green
Creed Haskins
Robert Jackson
Edward C. Smith
John Tucker
Burwell B. Wilkes
John Wyche

1833
Benj. D. Chapman
F. W. Green
John Manning
Wm. B. Meredith
W. Palmer
John Wyche

1834
Benj. D. Chapman
F. W. Green
John Manning
Wm. B. Meredith
John Tucker
John Wyche

1835
Wm. B. Meredith
Jos. A. Riddick
Burwell B. Wilkes

1836
Benj. D. Chapman
John Manning
Wm. Meredith
John Wyche

1837
Benj. D. Chapman
F. W. Green
John Manning
Wm. B. Meredith
Burwell B. Wilkes

1838
E. Hiram H. Blick
Benj. D. Chapman
F. W. Green
Wm. B. Meredith
Wm. H. E. Merritt
John Tucker
John Wyche

1839
F. W. Green
John C. Jones
Robert R. Jones
Wm. B. Meredith
Isham Trotter
Edward B. Tucker
E. R. (?) Tucker
John Wyche

1840
Daniel Hicks
Wm. B. Meredith
John Tucker
R. H. H. Wallton
Burwell B. Wilkes

1841
John P. Atkinson
F. W. Green
John C. Jones
Robert R. Jones
Joseph A. Riddick
Edward B. Tucker
John Wyche

1842
Benj. D. Chapman
R. W. Field
Wm. B. Meredith
Wm. H. E. Merritt
Edward B. Tucker
R. H. H. Wallton
Burwell B. Wilkes
John Wyche

1843
John P. Atkinson
Wm. H. E. Merritt
Joseph H. Travis
R. H. H. Wallton
Burwell B. Wilkes

1844
John P. Atkinson
J. B. Mallory
R. H. H. Wallton
Burwell B. Wilkes
John Wyche

1845
Wm. B. Meredith
R. H. Wallton
John Wyche

1846
John P. Atkinson
Burwell B. Wilkes

1847
J. B. Mallory
R. H. H. Wallton
Burwell B. Wilkes

1848
Wm. B. Meredith
Joseph A. Riddick
R. H. H. Wallton

1849
Wmsson Kelly
Luke J. Palmer
Joeph A. Riddick
R. H. H. Wallton
Burwell B. Wilkes

1850
R. H. H. Wallton

APPENDIX F
SCHEDULE OF FREE BLACK REGISTRATION

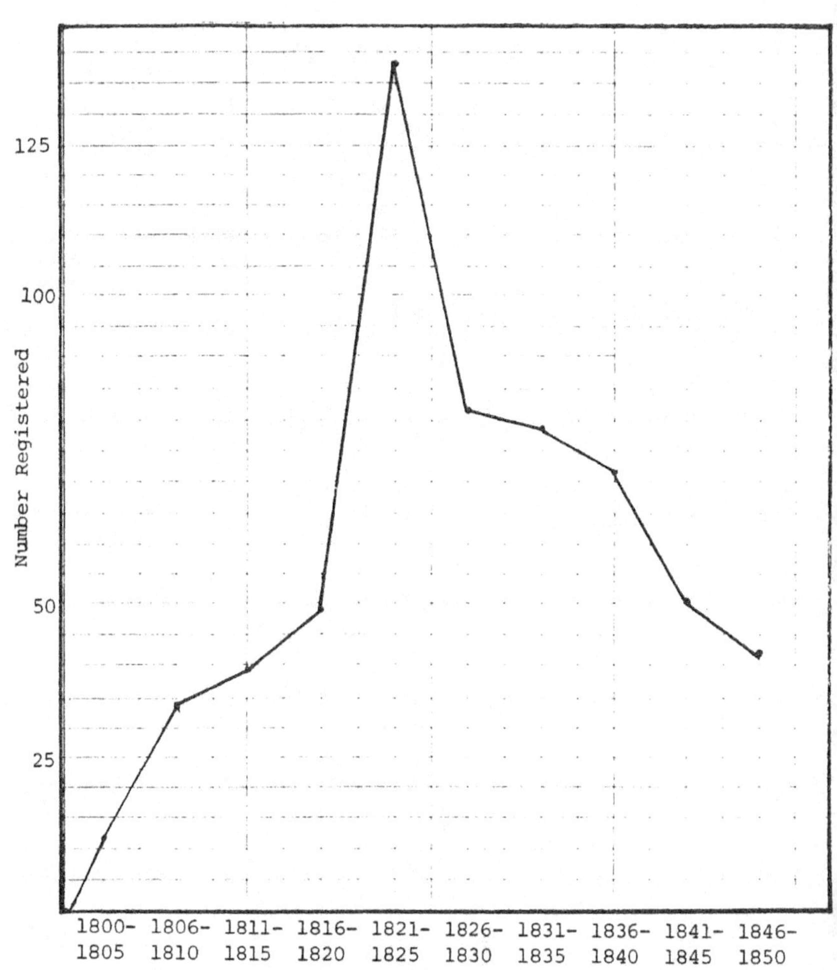

1 block = 5 registrants

1	1827	13
10	1828	35
1	1829	8
16	1830	8
2	1831	26
5	1832	21
2	1833	12
9	1834	12
6	1835	8
6	1836	11
14	1837	11
4	1838	17
9	1839	22
5	1840	11
8	1841	8
8	1842	11
5	1843	14
22	1844	11
36	1845	6
14	1846	7
56	1847	6
12	1848	8
19	1849	16
19	1850	5

APPENDIX G

ORIGINS of FREEDOM REFLECTED in REGISTRATIONS

	BOOK 1		BOOK 2		TOTAL	
	Number	Per cent*	Number	Per cent*	Number	Per cent*
Free Born	22	21	344	74	366	64
Last Will	33	31	50	11	83	15
Deed	35	33	52	11	87	15
Court	5	5	6	1	11	2
Unknown	10	10	12	3	22	4
Totals	105	100	464	100	569	100

* Rounded to nearest whole number

APPENDIX H

FORMATION of BRUNSWICK and CONTIGUOUS COUNTIES

and

BRUNSWICK COUNTY and NEARBY or ADJACENT NORTH CAROLINA COUNTIES

NAME	DATE CREATED	PARENT COUNTY	COUNTY SEAT
Brunswick	1720	Prince George, Isle of Wight, Surry	Lawrenceville
Dinwiddie	1752	Prince George	Dinwiddie
Greensville	1781	Brunswick, Sussex	Emporia
Isle of Wight	1634	Original Shire	Isle of Wight
Lunenburg	1746	Brunswick	Lunenburg
Mecklenburg	1764-5	Lunenburg	Boydton
Nottoway	1788-9	Amelia	Nottoway
Petersburg		Independent City	
Prince George	1702-3	Charles City	Prince George
Southampton	1749	Isle of Wight, Nansemond	Courtland
Surry	1652	James City	Surry
Sussex	1753-4	Surry	Sussex

Map of Brunswick County and Nearby or Adjacent North Carolina Counties

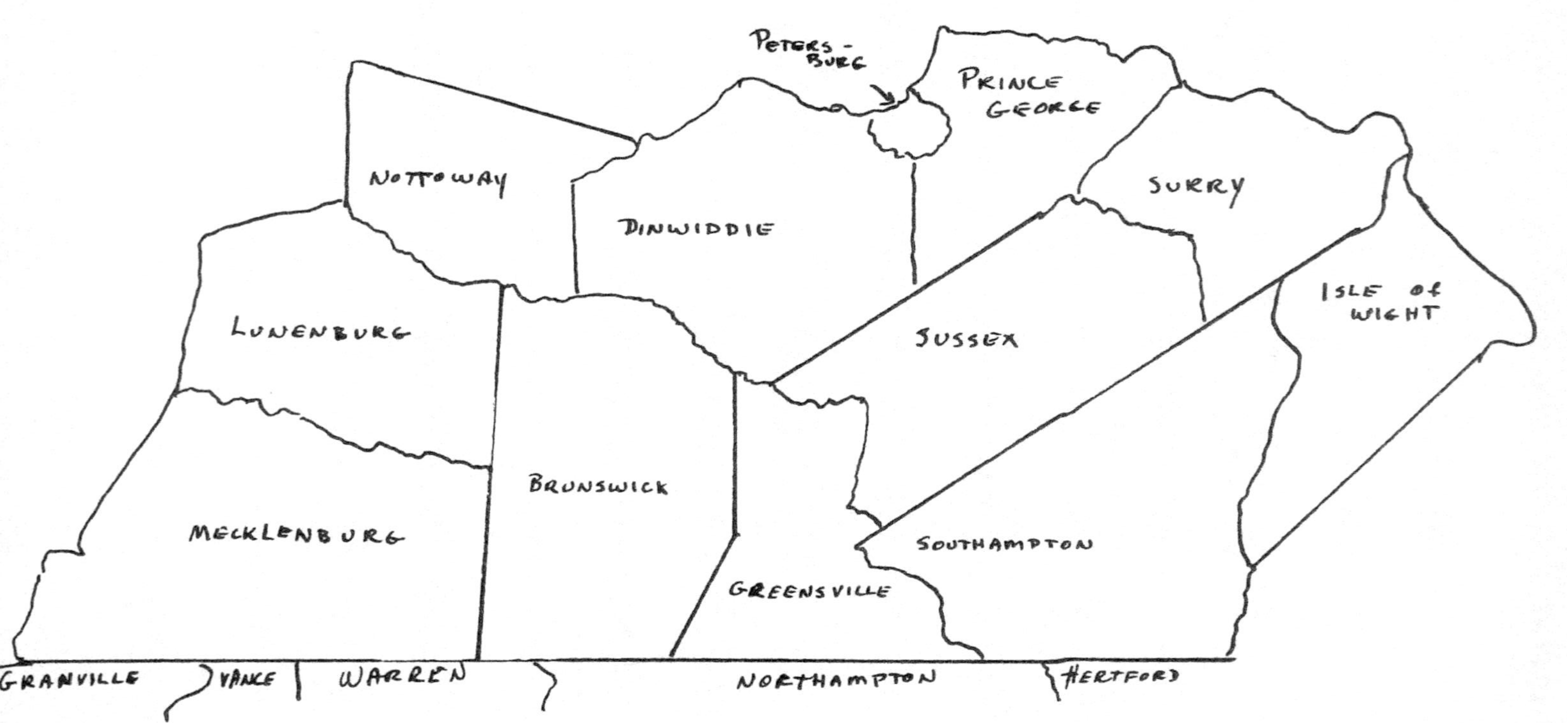

BIBLIOGRAPHY

Everton, George B., Sr., Ed., *The Handy Book for Genealogists,* Seventh Edition, The Everton Publishers, Inc., Logan, Utah, 1981.

Hening, William Waller, *The Statutes at Large; Being a Collection of All the Laws of Virginia, from the First Session of the Legislature in the Year 1619,* University Press of Virginia, Charlottesville, 1969.

National Archives and Records Service, *Third Census of the United States, 1810,* General Services Administration, Washington.

_______ *Fourth Census of the United States, 1830,* General Services Administration, Washington.

_______ *Fifth Census of the United States, 1830,* General Services Administration, Washington.

_______ *Sixth Census of the United States, 1840,* General Services Administration, Washington.

Shepherd, Samuel, *The Statutes at Large of Virginia, from October Session 1792, to December Session 1806, Inclusive, in Three Volumes, (New Series,) Being a Continuation of Hening,* AMS Press, Inc., New York, 1970.

Virginia State Travel Service, *Virginia Official State Highway and Transportation Map 1981,* Department of Highways and Transportation, Richmond, 1981.

I N D E X

www.ingramcontent.com/pod-product-compliance
Lightning Source LLC
LaVergne TN
LVHW050626100826
845148LV00011B/1754

* 9 7 8 0 7 8 8 4 2 7 6 3 3 *